The Lion That Swallowed Hemingway

A Literary Memoir

Orest Stocco

The Lion That Swallowed Hemingway

ISBN 978-0-9920112-8-4

Edited by Penny Lynn Cates
Cover Design by Penny Lynn Cates

"We all have a shadow. Or does our shadow have us? Carl Jung turned this question into a riddle when he asked: *'How do you find a lion that has swallowed you?'* Because the shadow is by definition unconscious, it is not always possible to know whether or not we are under the sway of some compelling part of our shadow's contents..."

MEETING THE SHADOW
The Hidden Power of the Dark Side of Human Nature

Edited by Connie Zweig and Jeremiah Abrams

"About posterity: I only think about writing truly. Posterity can take care of itself."

Ernest Hemingway

"The report of the shotgun in the morning quiet of the house on Wood River went echoing across the airwaves to every corner of the world. To the astonishment and dismay of many thousands of his admirers, the embattled old lion was dead. It was Sunday morning, July 2, 1961."

Hemingway: The Writer as Artist
Carlos Baker

Table of Contents

1. Back to Hemingway

That's how it started, my return to Hemingway, my high school hero who put a shotgun to his mouth and blew himself to hell as Nicholas Adams wanted to do to his own father in Hemingway's short story "Fathers and Sons," a movie that was about to play on television just as we were about to sit down for dinner: *Hemingway and Gellhorn,* starring Clive Owen as Ernest Hemingway and Nicole Kidman as his third wife, the writer Martha Gellhorn; the only one of his four wives to leave him.

"I'm sorry; I have to watch this movie," I said to Penny when she called me to the table. Our dinner guests, a friend from Toronto who had come up to her cottage for the weekend, and another friend and his new young Pilipino wife who lived down the street from us, stared at me. "It's a movie about Hemingway," I explained, and that was all I had to say for Penny to excuse my bad manners.

"I'll forgive you this time," she said, with that sweet smile that I had become familiar with the last few years ever since my open heart surgery which granted me the freedom to pursue my writing career, and she knew that Ernest Hemingway was as important to me as the other hero of my life, Carl Gustav Jung whose epic *Red Book* she had given to me for Christmas the year before and which I completely devoured before noon on New Year's day; a gift more precious than I could ever explain, but I will try as I relate this story of my return to Hemingway.

"Thanks love," I said, and set up a TV tray and made up a plate of baked ham, perogies, carrots, salad, fresh homemade rolls, and raisin pie for dessert.

"Hemingway is his favorite writer," Penny explained to our guests, who knew how passionate I was about writing and didn't really mind. Besides, our kitchen and sunken sunroom were one big room; so I'd only be a few feet away.

I turned the volume down but not too low and focused my attention on the story of Hemingway's tempestuous relationship with the wife who called her legendary husband a pathological liar and most self-centered man she knew; but despite his flaws (and by all accounts Hemingway had many) he had seized my imagination in high school and never stopped fascinating me.

Hemingway was a mystery. I didn't know if I could ever prove it, but I knew that that dried and frozen carcass of a leopard near the summit of Mount Kilimanjaro in "The Snows of Kilimanjaro," my favorite of all his short stories, symbolized Hemingway's paradoxical life, both the flawed man and gifted writer; and Harry, the flawed writer in the story, personified Hemingway's conflicted soul.

That's why I had to watch *Hemingway and Gellhorn*. But my need to watch the movie went beyond my fascination with my literary mentor; I felt compelled to watch it. On some deep pre-conscious gut level I *knew* that there was something about this movie that was going to give me answers to questions I had not even asked, like seeds waiting for the right conditions to sprout; and I was right.

"That's it!" I shouted half way through the movie. *"He had to have that to become a great writer!"* Everyone turned to look at me. *"Hemingway had to be a prick to become the great writer that he became!"* I exclaimed, unable to restrain the euphoria of my startling insight; and despite the smiles and puzzled stares, I knew I had just solved the mystery of the flawed man and gifted writer.

"Our life is choreographed," I said to Penny one morning over coffee in the bonus room above the double garage of our new house in Georgian Bay that I used for my writing den. "I'm more convinced of that every day."

Like Hemingway, every morning before the crack of dawn I go to my den to write; but unlike Hemingway, I don't do my writing standing up. And bonus room would be the perfect description for my writing den, because it is a bonus to have the time and freedom to write now; but I paid a dear price for my bonus time and freedom, both physically and emotionally.

I was called to be a writer. The idea of becoming a priest when I was an altar boy crossed my mind, but it didn't take hold; and by the time I finished grade eight I was reading a book a day because I could not get enough of reading. It was like I had a big hole in my soul and the only thing that could fill it was reading; and in high school I discovered literature, and Hemingway became my hero.

But it wasn't so much the writer that had seized my imagination, but the cocky young man whose courage to go out into the world to live his own life that took hold of me; a romantic ideal that appealed to many young writers, like Mordecai Richler and the incomparable short story writer Mavis Gallant who also went to Paris where Hemingway had forged out his apprenticeship under the tutelage of writers like Gertrude Stein and Ezra Pound and James Joyce which he sadly recounts in *A Moveable Feast* before shooting himself; but the writer and the man were one and the same person, and that's what made him the legend that he became.

I wish I would have had the courage to go out into the world and find my own writer's way like Ernest Hemingway; but that wasn't my destiny. I was born for another purpose, which was revealed to me when I read Somerset Maugham's novel *The Razor's Edge* in grade twelve. Larry Darrel, the hero of Maugham's novel, infected me with the seeker's virus; and despite all I did to cure myself by doing everything possible to avoid becoming a seeker, fate severed me from my life and I was forced to become a seeker like Maugham's intrepid soul-searching hero.

"I'm going away to look for answers that I know lie in my own back yard, but I have to go," I wrote in my journal (which proved to be more prophetic than I could ever imagine), and I left my pool hall and vending machine business behind me and

3

boarded an ocean liner in New York City bound for France to begin my own soul-searching quest for my true self like my fictional hero Larry Darrel.

But what happened to shift my priorities from wanting to become a writer to becoming a seeker? It wasn't Maugham's novel that changed my mind; that only sparked the fire of my need to find answers to my confused sense of self. Larry Darrel spoke to my confusion; that's why I became infected with the seeker's virus.

My confusion began in grade ten, and in grade twelve I identified with Larry Darrel's need for answers to the big questions of life; and although the virus didn't spike my fever for a few years, in my twenty-third year I had a sexual experience that so brutally shocked my conscience that it set the virus free and I had to go away to find my true self, because the person who did what he did that night was not the person I thought was me, and I vowed to find my true self or die trying.

I didn't go to France to become a writer, then; that was just an excuse to get away because everything in my hometown reminded me of what I had done, and I could not live with myself; but it took many years of questing to find out why I did what I did that godforsaken night, and it all started in grade ten with a mysterious change in my personality that began to confuse my sense of self.

I know now what happened to me, and I have the eminent psychologist C. G. Jung to thank because his insights into the human psyche gave me the understanding that I needed to make sense of my life, but I had to suffer my confusion for many years before I solved the baffling mystery of my *shadow* self.

The *shadow* is Jung's term for the repressed, unconscious side of our ego-personality; and everyone has a *shadow*. Our family has a *shadow*, and so does our religion, community, and our country. The *shadow* is everything that we don't want to be but are, only we are not aware of our *shadow* because we don't want to be conscious of what we don't want to be; and my high school hero had a monstrous *shadow* that seriously conflicted his ego-personality. That's what made Hemingway so damn exasperating to all his friends, and especially his last three wives.

The *shadow* is a mystery, and it takes great moral courage to see our *shadow* self; which is why we refuse to see the dark side of our personality, because if we do we have to take moral responsibility for it. But just because we aren't aware of our *shadow* self does not mean that it won't affect our behavior.

That's what Jung brought to my attention. His insight into the psyche made me see that my *shadow* was responsible for my confused sense of self that began in grade ten and continued for years until I learned to transform the dark *shadow* side of my personality with a teaching that I discovered at university where my quest had taken me when I came back home from France.

"A writer's job is to tell the truth," said my literary mentor, but the truth is much easier to tell in a work of fiction than it is in a memoir, because fiction gives a writer all the latitude that his imagination will allow; that's why Hemingway wrote fiction. His credo was to "tell it as it was," which he could not do if he stuck to the facts alone, so he had to make it up to tell the truth; but I can't. Memoir binds me to the facts of my life, so I don't have the luxury of making it up; I have to reserve that for my fiction, like my novel *Healing with Padre Pio,* an incredible story of my spiritual healing with an Ascended Master. Some of the facts of my life may be very hard to swallow, and there's not much I can do about that; but to tell it as it was I have to stick to the facts of my life and hope for the best. As I used to say in my aristocratic past lifetime in London, England, *"In for a penny, in for a pound."*

I lived in the Alpine city of Annecy in the *Haute Savoie* region of France for a year before I returned to Canada; but once again, this wasn't planned. It was choreographed from behind the scenes of life by what I came to call "the omniscient guiding force of life," which Hemingway called his creative "juice" and I finally came to identify simply as the Way. But this was long after I found the secret way of life in Gurdjieff's teaching and found my true self.

Something happened to me in Annecy that added so much fuel to the fire of my quest that I had to go where I was called to complete the next stage of my journey to my true self—to university to study philosophy; because what happened to me in Annecy set my confused mind ablaze with the "serpent fire."

The "serpent fire" is a metaphor for what some mystic traditions in the East call Kundalini, an untapped source of creative energy that exists in every person which when awakened from its primordial slumber can drive one out of his mind if one is not disciplined enough to sublimate it in a healthy and positive manner.

I awakened the "sleeping serpent" by accident one evening while practicing meditation for the first time in my life (students of Kundalini Yoga can meditate their whole life and not awaken the "sleeping serpent"), but I was not disciplined enough to tame it; and I was sucked into the illusionary world of my already confused mind where I could play out any fantasy of my desires, which were infinite in my insatiable egoic demands to be recognized; and it took ten years of remorseless "Gurdjieffian effort" to tame the energies of my awakened Kundalini.

But none of this would have happened had I not experienced that shadowy change in my personality in my second year of high school. Up to grade ten I was free to be my natural and spontaneous self, but somewhere in my tenth grade I underwent a metamorphosis in my personality that affected my behavior: I began to experience a very strange and irresistible impulse to be false.

It was the most uncomfortable feeling, and it always left me feeling guilty for what I had done, like I had committed an unpardonable sin against myself; but I couldn't help myself whenever the impulse possessed me, I *had* to pretend to be what I was not. And thus began the creation of a false persona that grew with every impulse to falseness that I submitted to, and in grade twelve this impulse to falseness erupted with *daemonic* fury in a poem that I wrote called "Noman" which so spooked my English teacher that he never looked at me the same way again.

Hemingway was also given to this strange impulse to falseness in his youth, as his many biographers have revealed (his grandfather said of the boy who loved to make up stories, "He's either going to be a great writer one day or end up in jail"), and it grew in direct proportion to his meteoric rise with the success of his first novel *The Sun Also Rises*; that's why his third wife called him a pathological liar and most self-centered man she knew. And near the end of his life the false *shadow* side of his personality took such control of his life that he killed himself to free himself of its tyranny, because Hemingway had to live life on his own terms or not at all.

Neither I nor Ernest Hemingway nor his doctors at the Mayo Clinic in Rochester who treated him with shock therapy for depression knew that it was our own dark, repressed *shadow* self that took possession of our personality; but as I watched my mentor and his wife play out the tempestuous drama of their relationship in *Hemingway and Gellhorn,* I caught a glimpse of what my other but invariably much more balanced hero Carl Gustav Jung called *"enantiodromia"*—the dynamic play of the opposing forces in our life; that's why I exclaimed, *"He had to have that to become a great writer!"*

In a sudden burst of illumination I realized that without the rapacious *shadow*-afflicted personality my high school hero would not have had the material to write such immortal works of fiction as "The Short Happy Life of Francis Macomber," "The Snows of Kilimanjaro," and the consummate work of his career, *The Old Man and the Sea*. Hemingway fed his *shadow* with his lust for life (he lived to hunt, fish, box, travel, drink, and have sex) and his *shadow* fed the creative genius of his art; and when the movie ended I went to my bookcase in our sunroom and took down *The Short Stories of Ernest Hemingway* and Carlos Baker's *Hemingway: The Writer as Artist*; and that's how I came back to Hemingway.

2. A Poem from the Depths

Writing is a mystical experience. Every writer knows this. They cannot explain how it works, but when it is working they know that they are in the presence of something holy, as the existential psychologist Rollo May said in his study of the creative process in *The Courage to Create*. And a writer has to write. He doesn't know why, but he simply has to write every day.

Doris Lessing, who like Hemingway garnered the Nobel Prize for Literature for her body of work, said in an interview that she could be gardening or doing whatever and be fully involved, but if she didn't write every day she felt that her day had been wasted, and she felt guilty and remorseful; why?

Hemingway wrote every day when he was working on a new story. He got up every morning despite how drunk he was the night before, and he wrote until he ran out of "juice" and/or knowing what was going to happen next in his story; but what drove him to write? What is it about writing that a writer has to write every day?

This mystery bothers writers, but they're much too busy writing to go out of their way to solve it; and the most they can say about it is that they seek truth through the stories they write, because through stories they get to the truth of life.

All writers know this, which Alice Munroe, who also won the Nobel Prize for Literature, summed up in her little gem of literary wisdom when she said: *"Memoir is the facts of life. Fiction is the truth of life."* So, is it the truth that drives writers to write every day? Is this why writers have to write; to get to the truth of life?

I was called to writing in my youth, but I didn't know why. Then something happened that shifted my priorities and I became a truth seeker instead; but I never stopped writing. In a way, I had two callings that worked together; but truth-seeking always came first, and I gave it my best and most creative energies.

But somewhere along the way (after studying dozens of different paths) my two paths of truth-seeking and writing merged into one personal path, and I discovered the secret that all writers wish to know—*why we are driven to write.*

It didn't happen overnight, mind you; it came as a slow realization that writing was an individual path to one's true self, and that all writers driven to write are on their own path to truth, which was why I came back to Hemingway. I had to re-read my high school hero to learn everything I could about his literary path to the truth of life, because the paradox of being a pathological liar and a writer whose job was to tell the truth fascinated the hell out of me; that's why I felt compelled to watch *Hemingway and Gellhorn,* because on some deeper level I knew that it would give me a clue to the mystery of Hemingway's enigmatic personality.

The clue came when I spontaneously erupted with, *"He had to have that to become a great writer!"* I don't know why I said that, but the drama of Hemingway's tempestuous relationship with Martha Gellhorn had focussed my attention enough for me to intuit that his paradoxical personality was responsible for his artistic genius; and then I exclaimed again, *"Hemingway had to be a prick to become the great writer that he became!"* because I *knew* with gnostic certainty that his *shadow* personality which frustrated the hell out of everyone, especially his third wife Martha whose journalistic integrity compelled her to tell the truth, was the unsolved mystery of Hemingway's literary path to the truth he sought through writing.

But as much as I had intuited this about the writer who had become my literary mentor, it would take months for my insight to work its way into a conceptual understanding; and that came when for some strange reason (this is why I've come to believe that our life is choreographed) I was strongly nudged to look up the strange word that popped into my mind which I had highlighted in Carl Jung's book *Modern Man In Search of a Soul* but had forgotten about, the word *"enantiodromia"* that Jung had coined to conceptualize the play of opposites in life and which he came to recognize as the central principle of our self-becoming as he studied the unconscious psyche of man.

It was strange that after all my years of reading Jung I had not explored this unpronounceable word which I began to realize was central to his psychology, because *enantiodromia* was the psychic engine that drove what Jung called the individuation process of our self-becoming, and the more research I did on *enantiodromia* the more Hemingway's paradoxical life fascinated me—because his whole life was one unending dynamic play of the *enantiodromiac* forces of his false *shadow* personality and his obsessive artistic integrity; and once I grasped the elusive principle of *enantiodromia* central to Jung's understanding of the individuation process, I *knew* (once again, in that intuitive gnostic way) that Hemingway's life symbolized this principle at the heart of every human experience—*which was the elusive truth of life that every writer sought with every story they wrote!*

I knew this intuitively; and it was my job to pull it out of myself just as a writer has to pull out from the depths of his creative unconscious the story that he has been inspired to write, like the writer John Irving who does not begin a new novel until he gets the first and last sentence of his story. Only then does he get to work of pulling out the story that lies between his first and last sentences.

That's what makes writing mystical. All of my stories come to me in a flash of synoptic insight, and then I have to pull them out of the deep recesses of my unconscious through the daily drudgery of working them out. That's why I e-mailed a friend of mine who was dismayed by my novel *Healing with Padre Pio* that had threatened the core of her spiritual certainty, "A writer does not choose the books he writes; they choose him." But only another writer would understand this.

Who or what then chooses the stories that a writer writes? What is this mysterious choreographer that I have come to call the omniscient guiding force that works behind the scenes of life, and why did it force the poem "Noman" out of me in high school that scared the pants off me and spooked my grade twelve English teacher whose idiosyncratic personality wasn't eccentric enough to fend off the *daemonic* passion of my mind-blowing mystical poem?

When I was fifteen I purchased an encyclopedic set of books called *The Great Books of the Western World,* which my eldest brother who worked at the paper mill had to sign for and which I paid in monthly instalments with my earnings spotting pins in a bowling alley and weekend job at the Hudson Bay grocery store, and in one of the study books to my accompanying set I read a poem by the Stoic poet Cleanthes that struck a chord but which took me many years to appreciate:

> Lead me Zeus,
> And thou, o destiny
> The way I am bid by thee to go.
> To follow I am willing,
> For were I recusant,
> I do but make myself a slave,
> And still must follow.

This is a simple poem with profound implications. It tells us that we all have a fixed destiny, and if we don't follow our destiny we're going to be dragged by it and suffer the consequences. I was dragged by my destiny; and it started with my high school poem "Noman" that erupted out of the depths of my unconscious.

Our prematurely grey-haired English teacher Mr. Mackay, whose right eye twitched whenever he got excited, a sure sign that he was either upset with us or up to another one of his weird assignments, asked the class to write a poem and he would select the best for the year book; and a week or so later I became possessed by "something" and my poem "Noman" erupted out of me like a volcano that had built up so much pressure it had to explode.

I now believe that this "something" that possessed me was my *daemon*, the archetypal spirit of my unconscious self; and my poem "Noman" was a message from my unconscious that foretold the destiny of my quest for my true self.

I didn't write this poem; it wrote itself. I merely held the pen in my puzzled hand as the words spewed out of me in a torrential flood of symbolic foretelling; and I know today that "Noman" would not have come pouring out of me had I not read the medieval play *The Summoning of Everyman* the week before writing my mystifying poem; but unfortunately I don't have a copy of "Noman," and all I remember are the last two lines that burned themselves into my memory.

Everyman, as the play is called today, is a medieval English morality play; and it touched my soul so deeply that my *daemon* woke me up to my situation, and one morning I jumped out of bed with an irrepressible urge to write a poem, and out came "Noman" in a flood of Biblical *thees* and *thous*. I was totally possessed by my *daemon*, and I experienced every single word that I wrote because I *was* Noman.

In the play *Everyman*, God sends his messenger Death to summon Everyman (every person in the world) for a reckoning; but Everyman is not ready to die, and he asks the Angel of Death for more time to prepare himself to meet God.

Death refuses, and Everyman panics. He asks his friends (symbolized in the person Fellowship) to accompany him, but Fellowship turns him down; then he asks his family (Kindred and Cousin), but they too refuse; and then he asks Goods (the material possessions that he has stored), but Goods refuses also.

Now desperate, Everyman asks Good Deeds, who wants to accompany him but cannot because he is too weak (symbolizing that Everyman had not done enough good deeds in his selfish life); but Good Deeds introduces Everyman to his sister Knowledge, who says she can help him by taking him to Confession. Everyman is so happy that he weeps with joy.

Confession tells Everyman that he will give him the precious gift of penance if he confesses his sins. Everyman calls upon the Lord to forgive his sins, and then Knowledge informs him that Good Deeds is strong enough now to accompany him, telling Everyman that he is now prepared for eternity; and Knowledge outfits Everyman with the robe of contrition to wear on his journey to eternity. The robe signifies repentance.

Good Deeds introduces Everyman to Discretion, Strength, his Five Wits, and Beauty and asks them to accompany Everyman on his journey. Knowledge then tells Everyman that he must receive the last sacrament of the Church, which he receives; and Discretion, Strength, Five Wits, and Beauty go with Everyman to his grave but refuse to accompany him to the afterlife. But Good Deeds says, "Nay, Everyman. I will bid with thee." Knowledge stays behind; only Good Deeds accompanies Everyman to the afterlife. And that's the parable of *Everyman*.

In my mystical poem, God's messenger informs Noman (which I came to learn many years later after I studied Jung was the *shadow* self of Everyman) that God wants a reckoning of Noman's life; and I'm brought to the Court of God, and God says to me in a voice that still reverberates in the chambers of my mind: "NOMAN, HAST THOU MY FISH'S SCALE?"

I answer no, and God sends me into the "abyss with four corners" to find the "fish's scale" and return it to God. But God imposes conditions. I have three days to search for the "fish's scale" in the "abyss with four corners," but it takes one whole day to search each corner of the "abyss," and if I do not find God's "fish's scale" in my allotted three days I will have failed because there would still be one corner left to search. So I go back into the world to search for the "fish's scale" (which I learned years later to mean my lost soul that belongs to God) in the first corner.

The four corners of the "abyss" symbolize the four points of the compass: North, South, East, and West; and they also, as I later came to see, symbolize the four planes of consciousness of the lower worlds of God—the Physical, Astral, Causal, and Mental Planes; and at the end of the first day I hear God's booming voice: "NOMAN, HAST THOU MY FISH'S SCALE?"

I answer that I do not have it, and I proceed to look in the second corner of the "abyss." I don't remember what I found in the first corner, nor in the second, but it wasn't my lost soul; and once again at the end of the second day God shouts: 'NOMAN, HAST THOU MY FISH'S SCALE?"

Again I say no, and then proceed to the third corner of the "abyss." Once again, I cannot remember what I found in the third corner (aside from a vague memory that had to do with my mother), but at the end of the third day God shouts again: "NOMAN, HAST THOU MY FISH'S SCALE?"

I do not have it, and I'm summoned back to God's Court. I tremble as I wait for God to pronounce judgement. God condemns me to the fourth corner of the "abyss" for eternity to find my lost soul, and as I fall from heaven I shout:

"Open you vile, voracious, loveable sweet whore!
God, why hast thou forsaken me?"

Thus ends the parable of "Noman," with me wandering throughout my little corner of the world in search of my lost soul; a poem that completely mystified me and spooked the hell out of my English teacher Mr. MacKay.

3. Literature Is Not Enough

Jungian analyst James Hillman wrote an insightful book called *The Soul's Code, In Search of Character and Calling*, which is about calling, fate, character, and image; and together they make up what Hillman called the "acorn theory," which holds that "each person bears a uniqueness that has to be lived and that is already present before it can be lived." This is the soul's code.

I believe in the soul's code, but not as James Hillman (nor Jung, for that matter) believed in it. They confined the "acorn theory" to one lifetime, entertaining the possibility that we may live more than one life but never publically embracing it; but I grew to believe in reincarnation from the day I discovered it in Plato's *Phaedo* and which was confirmed by at least three past-life recollection dreams that I had in high school, plus all of my extensive reading (especially on the "sleeping prophet" Edgar Cayce), and seven past-life regressions that I had when Penny and I relocated to cottage country in Georgian Bay, South Central Ontario.

So despite how much I wanted to become a writer in high school—which preoccupied me to the point of memorizing long lists of new words every week that I had to look up in all the books I read (this habit was inspired by James Joyce's *Portrait of the Artist as a Young Man*, because to understand writers like Joyce I had to expand my vocabulary) which led to an incident in one of my classes that alienated my English Literature teacher Mr. Mackay—my destiny was to find my soul, which I had no idea was even lost until I wrote my numinous poem "Noman."

One day in my English Literature class I used the word "juxtapose" in my response to something another student said, and Mr. MacKay, left eye twitching wildly, excitedly interjected with the full authority of all his learning, "There's no such word!

Juxtaposition is not a verb! It's a noun!" I nervously replied that it could also be used as a verb, and he told me to check the dictionary.

I did, and Mr. MacKay's white Irish face instantly turned the color of a lobster when thrown into a pot of boiling water, and he looked like a fool in front of his flummoxed class. I had a short sweet moment of egoic satisfaction, but I paid for it dearly down the road; so it seemed that the forces behind the scenes of life were working to align my life with my destiny of finding my lost soul by pulling me away from writing, and then I read *The Razor's Edge* and my fate was sealed.

But I still wanted to become a writer, and I wrote a weekly article under my by-line "Teen Talk" for my hometown newspaper which if memory serves me was called *The Nipigonoose*. But several months after I began writing my articles I got a phone call from the editor of *The Chronicle Journal* in Port Arthur, Fort William's twin city (the two cities would eventually unite to become the city of Thunder Bay), asking if I would write a weekly article for their daily paper; but in my foolish sense of loyalty to the publisher of our small-town newspaper, I declined the offer.

When Hemingway was fresh out of high school he began his writing career with the *Kansas City Star* where he worked for seven months and learned how to write short vigorous sentences and avoid the use of adjectives, especially extravagant ones, a style that he honed to a fine art that has been emulated by countless writers ever since; and when he came back from Italy where he drove ambulance for the American Red Cross on the Italian front and was severely wounded by an Austrian mortar shell and machine gun fire, an experience that inspired some of his best short stories and his novels *The Sun Also Rises* and *A Farewell to Arms*, he wrote for the *Toronto Daily Star* and *Star Weekly*; so who knows where writing could have taken me had I followed up on *The Chronicle Journal's* offer?

My "acorn" was encoded with my destiny to find my lost soul, and despite how much I tried to avoid my soul's call by forging a life in business at the age of twenty-one by operating the pool hall in my hometown of Nipigon, which I expanded to include pin ball and cigarette vending machines that I had consigned in several restaurants, I was rudely severed from my entrepreneurial life with a sexual experience that brutally shocked my conscience awake and catapulted me into my quest for my true self; I sold my business investment and went to France.

Everyone thought I was crazy, especially my family, and they were probably right; but when one is caught in the grips of his *daemonic* spirit he cannot help himself. And to further confuse my life, I accidentally opened up the chakra at the base of my spine in Annecy while meditating on a maple leaf one night and awakened the "coiled serpent" from its primordial slumber and set it free to crawl up the canal of my spine with a tickling sensation where it lodged itself into my brain and set my mind on fire with every imaginable desire; and trying to harness the wild energies of the "serpent fire" could have driven me out of my mind had I not found a teaching that saved me from the erotic fantasies of my private life.

In my second year at university a fellow philosophy student was going home for Christmas and out of the blue asked if he could pick up a book for me from his favorite second-hand book store in Toronto. I didn't have any book in mind, so I asked him to surprise me; and he brought me back a book that set my feet firmly on my destined course: *In Search of the Miraculous, Fragments of an Unknown Teaching*, by P. D. Ouspensky, a former student of a strange man called Gurdjieff who founded a mystery school called *The Institute for the Harmonious Development of Man* in Fontainebleau-Avon near Paris at the same time that Hemingway and other expatriate writers were living in Paris and where Margaret Anderson, who published some of Hemingway's stories in her magazine *The Literary Review* as well as parts of Joyce's controversial novel *Ulysses*, had also gone to study Gurdjieff's teaching because she too had come to the sad realization that literature was not enough to nourish her soul, along with her partner Kathryn Hulme, the author of *Undiscovered Country, In Search of Gurdjieff* and her autobiographical novel *The Nun's Story* that was made into a movie starring Audrey Hepburn.

The gifted New Zealand short story writer Katherine Mansfield who was dying of tuberculosis also went to the Gurdjieff Institute because she had come to the same soul-numbing realization that literature was not enough to satisfy the longing in her soul, as she expressed it to A. R. Orage, her literary mentor and editor of the *New Age* journal in London, England who had published some of her stories; and she thought as did Orage, who sold his *New Age* journal and went to the Institute also, that Gurdjieff's teaching would give them what they needed to satisfy the longing in their soul that literature could no longer give them.

Many writers and artists went to study under Gurdjieff at his infamous Institute in Fontainebleau-Avon, and they were known in Paris as "the forest philosophers," but it didn't matter that Gurdjieff was thought to be a charlatan by the Parisian literati, what I read in Ouspenksy's book resonated so deeply with me that I knew intuitively that this teaching would save me from myself; and in my third year I dropped out of university to continue my quest for my lost soul in the school of hard knocks with Gurdjieff's remarkably teaching of "work on oneself."

"There is only self-initiation into the mysteries of life," said Gurdjieff; and had I not initiated myself into the mystery of the Kundalini I would never have come to appreciate the unbelievably creative energy of the "serpent fire," and I have proof of my initiation experience: after I did the meditation that accidentally opened up the chakra at the base of my spine and awakened the Kundalini, I recorded my experience in the blank front and back covers of a paperback copy of Emily Bronte's novel *Wuthering Heights* that I was reading at the time.

I dated my Kundalini-awakening experience October 21, 1968; and I was only twenty-three years old when I accidentally put my sanity in dangerous risk. I didn't know what Kundalini was, nor did I have the requisite vocabulary to express myself; but I wrote down what happened the best way I knew how:

Tonight I think I have experienced meditation in its truest form. How and why I will explain. I had been reading a book, Concentration: An Approach to Meditation; *and in it I read that to meditate one must so to speak become harmonious with what he is meditating on. The example it gave was a flower. It said to observe the flower very carefully the next time you passed a flower. To stop, pick up the flower, observe it, feel it, smell it, note its colors, its texture, everything about the flower, and then when you want to meditate, in your moment of tranquility to pick that beautiful little flower as your object of meditation.*

Well, I did this; only with a leaf. By sheer accident yesterday when I was waiting for the kids (Sabrina and Patricia, my new friend's young daughters) to come out of school I happened to pick up a fallen maple leaf. I fiddled around with it for a while, and then what I had read about the flower came to me, and I observed the leaf as closely as I could. I noted its color, its texture, its size, shape, and even its odor, and the conclusion I came to was that it was beautiful. It really was beautiful. I did not want to throw it away. I wanted to keep it forever and ever. I wanted it. I cherished it. I loved it. I loved a leaf! But then I thought of the absurdity of it all, and still I clung to it. I did not want to throw it away, and I did not until the young girls came out of school, for it was then that being forced by the sheer reality of our difference, because as I gave Sabrina and Patricia a kiss on the cheek I let it slip hesitantly from my hand and quickly grasped the girls' hands, one on each side, to get in touch with real people, real existence, and yet I could not stop feeling that that beautiful little leaf did have an existence of its own and that I had come to realize it. Now I believe it has. Here is what happened:

I was sitting alone reading, and it was very quiet except for the ticking of a clock. Then the idea struck me to try meditation on that leaf I had so perspicaciously observed. I must note here that when I observed the leaf it was smooth and waxy on one side and the other was not so smooth owing to the veins which projected from the main stem to all the extremities of the leaf. And the stem was fine and thin on its attachment but thickened progressively as it neared its creator, and when the wind had separated it how there remained a slight yet noticeable hole which I made a note of recollecting at the time because if ever I was to meditate on that leaf my existence would become harmonious with its existence via this golden gate, and so I assumed the position directed in the book to sit with my feet flat on the floor, my back as straight as comfort would allow, my hands resting on my knees and my head straight and my eyes looking straight ahead, and slowly I began to meditate on the leaf.

I began my meditation by observing first its size, shape, and form, and I viewed it mentally from all angles, up, down, sideways, frontwards, backwards, and then I observed its color, texture, and odor; then all my observations were meditated upon simultaneously with a center of concentration upon the golden gate. I concentrated and concentrated, and as I did so I repeated such lines to myself: "How beautiful you are. I want to be you. I want my existence to be your existence. I want that we should be one and the same. We will be harmonious." And as I repeated these lines I pictured my "self," my existence (and it was not normal, for I pictured my existence as shapeless, formless, without creation, as though it was the "me" of me) enter the golden gate slowly, very slowly, and as I began to enter my back began to stiffen, and the deeper my existence went into the existence of the leaf the more rigid my back became and the lighter my head felt, and the lighter it felt the more it began to float, and as the "me" of me entered into the veins of the leaf I felt a certain physical levitation which was climaxed by a certain mental euphoria as the "me" of me touched every extremity of the leaf and became one and the same as the "it" of it. I consciously felt, for I had not by any means lost my powers of reason for I was still conscious of what was going on because deep down somewhere I knew it was just an experiment, but nevertheless I consciously felt a symbiosis, a union with the "me" and the "it" united to make "one". This had such a physical effect on me that the stiffening of my back and the weightlessness of my head, as though it wanted to leave the body and float away somewhere, snapped me into, so to speak, the materialistic reality of it all that it sent a momentary chill through me and in order for me to get back into the swing of things I decided to relinquish the experiment, but I did this carefully also.

I slowly withdrew my existence—the "me" from the "it" via the same means of entry, and curiously enough as I did this my back began to lose the rigidity it experienced and my head the weightlessness, and the further the "me" withdrew the more normal I became until when the "me" was completely removed and inharmonious with the "it" I felt the way I had begun my meditation, tranquil, phlegmatic, yet somehow thwarted.

Is it possible that my *daemon* (what the ancient Romans referred to our "inner genius") knew that literature was not enough and pulled me away from a life of writing because I would need something more than literature to find my lost soul and awakened the sleeping "serpent" to fuel my quest for my true self?

Shakespeare, Wordsworth, Rumi—all great poets whose genius reflected the inherent wisdom of life (I was to model my life on Wordsworth's poem "Character of the Happy Warrior" one day); but they weren't enough to satisfy my desperate longing for my true self. Is that why the redoubtable Gurdjieff came into my life?

Without Gurdjieff's teaching to focus my attention, the Kundalini energy could have easily destroyed my life as it has so many others; but because his teaching was tailor-made to harness the energies of my life (both inner and outer), I had no more reason to study philosophy; so I left university and went out into the world to "work" on myself with his teaching and begin what Jung, who was to become the other hero of my life, called my "confrontation with the unconscious." That's how life became my classroom, and experience my hard-knocks teacher which would one day lead be right back to my high school hero, Ernest Hemingway.

4. Hemingway's Credo

"No other writer of our time has so fiercely asserted, so pugnaciously defended, or so consistently exemplified the writer's obligation to speak truly," said Carlos Baker in *Hemingway: The Writer as Artist.*

In effect, all of Hemingway's writing was born of his own life experience; which is why his literary credo was to "tell it the way it was." But what if one's experience is "out there"? What if one's experience is outside the range of the average person's life; like having an out-of-body experience, for example?

This is the dilemma that every writer will have to face one day, because there is no such thing as an average person; every person's life is unique, and every person will one day have an experience that's "out there."

Hemingway did, and he had to deal with it; but he was clever enough to deal with it in a way that didn't seem "out there," as such; he wove it into the context of his stories with such skillful ease that he made it seem normal. "You have to take what is not palpable," said my mentor in a letter to Bernard Berenson, "and make it completely palpable and also have it seem normal and so that it can become a part of the experience of the person who reads it" (*Selected Letters*, p. 837).

When driving ambulance on the Italian front Hemingway was severely wounded, which over time his impulse to falseness compelled him to exaggerate and make much more of his war experience than what had actually happened because there was no glory in telling the world that he was delivering cigarettes and candy bars to the fighting soldiers on the front line when he was wounded by an Austrian trench mortar shell and machine gun fire; but as he lay on the ground dying he slipped out of his body and floated above his mortal coil long enough to see himself badly wounded and then he returned to his body, and though Hemingway never really believed it he was told that he carried another wounded soldier to safety and for his act of bravery was awarded the Italian Silver Medal of Valor.

He was conscious of leaving his body, but he did not want to make his OBE (out-of-body experience) public knowledge because it was one of those strange experiences that would be too "out there" for anyone to believe; but it happened to him, and he had an obligation to tell it the way it was when he wrote about his war experience, which he did in his novel *A Farewell to Arms* and in one of his Nickolas Adams stories. He wove his out-of-body experience into his novel and short story "Now I Lay" so seamlessly that he made it palpable.

Thank goodness I recorded my Kundalini experience immediately after it happened, so I know that it wasn't an emotionally induced fantasy, or a dream. I told it the way it was to the best of my ability; and I'm glad I did because that experience was responsible for everything that happened to me after I awakened the "sleeping serpent," which gave my *daemon* what it needed to pull a teaching into my life that would help me realize my destiny and find my lost soul. That's what I mean when I say that our life is choreographed by an invisible force behind the scenes of life; but it's a two-way dynamic, because we create the opportunities for the guiding force of life to come into play and assist us in realizing our destiny to our true self.

The target draws forth the arrow, as it were; the target being my destiny, and the arrow being Gurdjieff's teaching. This reconciles the paradox of our free will with the fixed will of our destiny; exactly what Cleanthes meant by his poem. But it would take years before I discerned the nuances of my quest for my true self.

So I knew how difficult it would be to tell it the way it was, because my life was nothing like my literary mentor's. Hemingway lived to live. His life was all about experiencing as much of life as he could before dying. He stared into the face of death on the Italian front and wanted to pack as much experience into his short life as he could so he could write about it, that's why he jumped in with both feet whenever life grabbed his attention—like bullfighting.

Hemingway's first novel *The Sun Also Rises* was inspired by his wild fiesta experience with friends in Pamplona where they had gone to see the running of the bulls; so fascinated did the young writer become with the total experience of bullfighting that he became an obsessed aficionado and would later write what some critics considered to be the best book on bullfighting, *Death in the Afternoon*, followed many years later by *A Dangerous Summer*.

That's how Hemingway was with everything that he did—fishing for trout in upper Michigan, bird and small game hunting, deep sea fishing, big game hunting in Wyoming and Africa, bullfighting, boxing, horse-racing, drinking, and having sex. How he loved to make love with other women when he got tired of his wives, and in ways that he never revealed but implied in his writing, like his novel *The Garden of Eden* that was published posthumously, and with good reason.

My life was radically different. I did not live to live; I wanted to find an answer to the riddle of my confused life. I was on a quest to find my lost soul, not gorge myself on life like the great Ernest Hemingway; but still, I had to live my life.

One night in Annecy I had a dream with my high school hero. Hemingway came to me in my dream. I was sitting at my desk working on my first novel, which I called *This Petty Pace*, inspired by Macbeth's famous soliloquy: "Tomorrow, and tomorrow, and tomorrow, /Creeps in this petty pace..." Hemingway stood a few feet away from me, like he was stalking me; and he made me feel uneasy.

His beard was white and he looked like the grizzled Papa Hemingway of his late-life photos, and his beady eyes studied me so intently that I felt like a wild beast caught in the sight of the barrel of his gun, and with a bluntness that startled me he said, "I have pissed out more life than you have lived," and with a big smirk on his face he walked away and I felt like I had just been mortally wounded.

I didn't grasp immediately what he meant by his one-shot comment; but it soon became apparent that he was telling me in that symbolic language that Carl Jung put me wise to many years later that I had to go out and live my life before I could write about life with the authority of authenticity; but my dream message went much deeper than that, because it went to the core of the human experience that I was trying to capture in *This Petty Pace*—was life a tale told by an idiot full of sound and fury signifying nothing; or *nada,* as Hemingway tried to express the hollow in his own soul in one of his most popular stories, "A Clean, Well-lighted Place"?

Hemingway spoke to the eternal mystery of life, to that essential truth that he could never quite grasp but sought with passionate intensity with every experience that he had; and if he could not experience it in real life, he experienced it in the stories that he imagined, like Colonel Richard Cantwell's romantic infatuation with the eighteen-year old Venetian girl called Renata in his novel *Across the River and into the Trees* that was inspired by his own obsessive fascination with the flesh and blood nineteen year-old aristocratic beauty Adriana Ivancich from Venice, Italy. That was another reason why Hemingway *had* to write; he had to have it all, any which way he could—including his sexual fetishes that every one of his wives became aware of eventually, and some other women as well.

But try as he may, Hemingway never quite grasped the secret of life that he was after despite his creative genius and passionate involvement with life. As he said to his fourth and longsuffering last wife Mary Welsh, whom she quotes in the embarrassingly candid memoir of her life with the great writer, ironically titled *How It Was* (giving her the last word on her alcoholic husband who called her "whore, bitch, liar, moron," and other unforgivably cruel names when he was caught in the pitiless jaws of his bestial *shadow*): "Nobody really knows or understands and nobody has ever said the secret. The secret is that it is poetry written into prose and it is the hardest of all things to do."

The secret of life that is poetry but which even the poets in all their genius can only hint at was what I was after; but not by experiencing all the life that I could and then write about it like Hemingway, because like Katherine Mansfield and the editor of the *New Age* journal who published such gifted writers as George Bernard Shaw, H. G. Wells, T. S. Eliot and others, I knew deep down in that unconscious way that drove my quest with *daemonic* ferocity that literature was not enough.

That's why I became a seeker. I had to find the meaning of my life; and I took to Gurdjieff's teaching with such pathological commitment that I transformed my consciousness and experienced the secret that all the writers and artists were after—the mystical union of our two selves that I would spend the rest of my life trying to articulate in my own writing, like my novels *Keeper of the Flame* and *Jesus Wears Dockers* and my new book of short stories that was set free by my unexpected return to Hemingway who re-inspired my writing because I had lived my life and could write about it now with an authority that would wipe that arrogant smirk off his face when he took his pot-shot at me in my dream forty-six years ago in Annecy.

To do it the justice that it deserved, I had to frame the story of my life in the genre of fiction. That was the only way I could tell it the way it truly was, just as Francisco Goldman said about his novel *Say Her Name*. Goldman's novel was about his talented young writer wife Aura Estrada, who was fatally injured by a freak wave when they were vacationing on the Coast of Mexico and which his mother-in-law blamed him for; when asked by the *Paris Review* why he wrote his obviously autobiographical story as a novel and not memoir, he replied: *"I made things up in order to be able to tell the truth"*—because he had to employ his imagination to explore all the nooks and crannies of his relationship to get to the truth of his love for his beautiful wife and her unexpected, tragic death.

That's what Hemingway did with the novel that launched his career; he made things up to get as close to the truth of his experience as his imagination would allow. That's what the poet Adrienne Rich meant when she said, *"Poetry is an act of the imagination that transforms reality into a deeper perception of what is."* This applies to prose as well, and Hemingway engaged the evocative powers of his imagination to create a deeper perception of his experience with his friends in Pamplona; but he pissed a lot of people off, because the models for his thinly disguised characters in *The Sun Also Rises* identified themselves and never forgave him for his betrayal of their friendship, especially Harold Loeb who forty years later was still smarting from the way Hemingway had portrayed him in the character of the sycophantic Robert Cohn; and that happened to me also, but in spades.

I pissed off a whole community with my first novel *What Would I Say Today if I Were to Die Tomorrow?* I created such a deep perception of my community that the whole town identified with the *shadow personality* of my hometown that I had the temerity to magnify with my imagination in my novel, and Penny and I had to relocate to Georgian Bay for peace of mind; so I understand how writers feel when they chafe people who identify with the characters modeled on their life; but is that fair to the author and the people who inspire their fictional characters?

I've given this a lot of thought since I wrote *What Would I Say Today if I Were to Die Tomorrow?* And try as I may, I cannot blame the writer for modelling his characters on real people to get to the truth of life, because to create a deeper perception of what *is* a writer has to capture the essence of his characters, and he needs real life models because they manifest the archetypal essence of their unique individuality; and more often than not a writer needs the essential spirit of more than one real person to create a composite character that his story is calling for to ferret out the truth the writer is after. This is the mystical nature of creative writing.

Ironically however, characters in a work of fiction are NOT their real-life models; they are their own person. But this is so difficult to understand that a writer can argue until he is blue in the face and no one will believe him. "You're just justifying yourself," they all say; but not so. Why do you suppose, for example, some characters appear complete with their own life history in a writer's mind?

Every writer has a special relationship with their creative unconscious, despite the end result of their work; and although most writers have to work like hell to create their characters, some writers are blessed with the gift of accessing their creative unconscious with an ease that is the envy of most writers, like Mavis Gallant whose short stories have graced the pages of *The New Yorker* for many years. Which is not to say that she did not work hard on her stories; she labored like few writers have worked to make her stories as close to perfect as possible. But like she tells us in a documentary video on *The Writing of Mavis Gallant*, her special gift was to be open to the stories that her creative unconscious provided for her:

"The first flash of fiction arrives without words. It consists of a fixed image, like a slide, or closer still, a fixed frame showing characters in a single situation. Every character comes into being with a name, which I may change, an age, a nationality, a profession, a particular voice and accent, a family background, a personal history, a destination, qualities, secrets, an attitude towards love, ambition, money, religion, and with a private center of gravity. After the first idea of a story and your first sort-of vision of people in it, the next thing that comes, perhaps a couple of days later, is a flow of dialogue. They speak, and I don't hear the exact words—I don't know how to explain this. I'm trying to explain something that can't be explained, but I know what they're talking about and I know what they're saying, even if it's in another language I know what they're saying, or whatever..."

If these characters came to Mavis Gallant with a complete history, where did they come from? They had to come from somewhere. Did they come from her imagination? That's what

29

we would like to believe; but that doesn't explain the mystery of their origin. Mavis Gallant did not know these people. They came to her complete unto themselves, and it was her job as a writer to tell their story.

The closest that I can come to explaining this is that these imaginary people are archetypes that come from what Jung called the collective unconscious (Jung met some of these archetypal people when he had his confrontation with the unconscious that he recorded in *The Red Book*); and a writer who has the gift of being open to the creative unconscious gives these archetypes the freedom to live out their life in the writer's mind which he/she then write into their stories.

As Jung was told by one of the people that he met when he descended into the depths of his own unconscious, a Gnostic Master by the name of Philemon, he was real, as were everyone that Jung met in the unconscious. They were real and had an independent existence separate from his own mind; so it doesn't surprise me to learn that some characters come full-blown as they did to Mavis Gallant.

That never happened to me; but I can speak to the experience of my fictional characters taking on their own life once I ensouled them with the archetypal spirit of the people they were modeled on. This is why I can say in all good conscience that the fictional characters in a writer's story have their own independent existence separate from the life of their models. Their real life models simply ensoul the fictional characters, not unlike a father and mother creating their own child that has a life independent of its parents. The child is both of its parents, but it is also a separate person independent of its parents; and so are a writer's fictional characters.

This is why James Joyce called writers gods who create their own kingdom with each story they write, and telling it the way it was involves much more than people realize because it is a magical insemination of imagination with reality. As my literary mentor said in *Bi-Line: Ernest Hemingway*: "It is one thing beside honesty that a good writer must have. The more he learns from experience the more truly he can imagine. If he gets so he can imagine truly enough people will think that the things he relates all really happened and that is just reporting."

But as the novelist Karen Blixen said, this kind of reporting is art, "the truth above the facts of life." And that's the heart of Hemingway's credo.

5. The Way According to Hemingway

By the time Carl Jung turned forty he had achieved everything that he had wished for himself—"honor, power, wealth, knowledge, and every human happiness." Then his desire for the increase in these trappings ceased, and a horror came over him. "My soul, where are you?" asks Jung; and thus began his descent into his unconscious in search of his lost soul.

Jung chronicled his quest for his lost soul in four black notebooks that he later transcribed into what he called *The Red Book*, and when Penny gave me A Reader's Edition of *The Red Book* for my Christmas gift I dove into it instantly; and as difficult as it was to read (most readers take months to read *The Red Book*), I had completely devoured it before nine o'clock New Year's Day.

From the very first page Jung's quest for his lost soul grabbed my attention and never let up. Jung addresses his soul, asking it where it has gone. He was so busy pursuing "honor, power, wealth, knowledge, and every human happiness" that he forgot about his soul, and now he felt lost without it; that's why he asks, "My soul, where are you?" But now Jung is back. He has shaken the dust off his feet and has returned, and he says to his soul: "But one thing you must know: the one thing that I have learned is that one must live this life. This life is the way, the long sought-after way to the unfathomable, which we call divine. There is no other way, all other ways are false paths" (*The Red Book*, Reader's Edition, pp. 127-8).

This spoke to me. I knew with gnostic certainty that Jung was speaking the truth, and I couldn't wait to immerse myself in his quest for his lost soul; and when I came to the last page and Philemon asks Jesus what he has brought, Jesus replies (and this is the last line of Jung's chronicle): "I bring you the beauty of suffering. That is what is needed by whoever hosts the worm."

With these words I was given a synoptic vision and instantly knew that I would one day write a book called "The Beauty of Suffering." But whether I write this book or not depends upon many things; the important thing is that I caught the essential meaning of Christ's words, and I knew what Jesus meant by the beauty of suffering. I had come to the realization that suffering was nature's way of driving the *enantiodromiac* process of man's individuation, and the premise of my book would be to articulate why suffering was merciful and necessary for humanity.

I'm not one to cry, "Why me, God?" I know that we are the authors of our own karmic destiny, and I don't cry foul whenever misfortune befalls me; that's why when Jung confessed to his soul that one must live this life because this life is the way, I embraced his truth because it mirrored my own life; and I read, and read, and read until Jesus revealed that suffering was necessary for all those who host the worm; that's why suffering was beautiful and not a tale told by an idiot full of sound and fury signifying nothing, because through suffering we transform the ugliness of our worm (which Jung identified as our *shadow* self) into beauty (which Jung identified as our archetypal Self); this is why this life is "the long sought-after way to the unfathomable, which we call divine."

And this is why I loved Hemingway. He had the courage to go out and live his own life, no matter the suffering it would cost him; and then write about it. As he said to his friend and writer F. Scott Fitzgerald, "Forget your personal tragedy. We are all bitched from the start and you especially have to be hurt like hell before you can write seriously. But when you get the damned hurt use it—don't cheat with it. Be as faithful to it as a scientist—but don't think anything is of any importance because it happens to you or anyone belonging to you" (*Ernest Hemingway on Writing*, edited by Larry W. Phillips, pp. 19-20).

Hemingway knew that this life was the way. He didn't have a mystical awareness that this life was the way; he knew instinctively, as many people who have the courage to go out and live their own life do. They have a need to live their own life to satisfy that endless longing in their soul to be their own person—whether they believe they have a soul or not, which Hemingway did. He also believed that animals have souls; but he was not a religious man—unless it served his needs, that is. Like the time he became impotent and went to church and prayed to God and then went home and made love with Pauline like they had just invented sex.

Hemingway was an existentialist. Not a philosophical existentialist like Jean Paul Sartre who studied Hemingway's work and visited him at his home in Cuba because he embodied Sartre's philosophy of the man condemned to be freely himself; Hemingway was a living example of someone who existed to live, not lived to exist. The last thing that Hemingway wanted was for his life to be a "useless passion," and he did not squander his life on what did not interest him. That's why he made a point of getting as much enjoyment out of life as he could, whatever the cost; and the most tragic cost was his marriage to the woman who at the end of his life-weary life he revealed to be the one true love of his life. "I wish I had died before I ever loved anyone but her," he confessed in *A Moveable Feast.*

But it was his choice to betray Hadley and have an affair with their rich and fashionable friend Pauline Pfeiffer who insinuated her way into their happy marriage and betrayed her friend Hadley to become Hemingway's second wife. He could have chosen not to have an affair, but he had to have Pauline; that was his nature. He was a hapless servant of his needs, and he grabbed life whenever it presented itself, and it didn't matter that he hurt others. He was out to get what he could however he could get it to satisfy his *daemon* and be the best writer of his generation which he could only do by experiencing all the life he could so he could write about it truly.

This is how Hemingway fueled the *enantiodromiac* process of his own individuation; he grew into the great writer that he wanted to be by feeding the dialectic of his own becoming with his *daemonic* lust for new experiences, which invariably ended up hurting everyone close to him; especially his four wives.

Somewhere along the way Hemingway made his life his first priority, and everything else came second; probably because he did not want to end up like his father who cowered to his wife Grace whom Ernest hated with a passion (General Buck Lanham, one of Hemingway's closest friends, said that Ernest was the only person he knew who truly hated his mother); and my high school hero was true to himself to the bittersweet end of his tragic life. But he would not have become a great writer had he not been driven by his *daemon* to write, which was his destined purpose; and that's where Hemingway and I parted company.

My *daemonic* destiny was to become a seeker first, and then a writer; and my first priority was to find my true self whatever the cost. In that way Hemingway and I were alike; but where Hemingway fed his *shadow* through his passion for life, I sought to find my *shadow* out because I knew that the dark *shadow* side of my personality was not the real me. It was who I was not, the unconscious potential self of my becoming; and when I discovered Gurdjieff's teaching I made it my mission to transform the insidious worm in me and become my true self.

That's how I gravitated to what Jung called "the secret way of life" that Jesus couched in his cryptic sayings and which I explored in my novels *Jesus Wears Dockers* and *St. Paul's Conceit*. That's how I came to appreciate what Jesus meant by "the beauty of suffering," which he symbolized in his gift to the world with his death upon the cross; but my high school hero didn't see suffering that way. For Hemingway suffering was a natural part of life that had to be dealt with, and with as much dignity as possible; which was why he fell in love with bullfighting.

Hemingway saw the whole drama of life and death in the bullfight; and the more grace the matador displayed in the ring, the more Hemingway admired and respected him. Perhaps this gave birth to his motto, "grace under pressure," which he tried his whole life to live up to and which he amplified with creative genius in "The Short Happy Life of Francis Macomber," because Macomber salvaged his dignity moments before his bitch of a wife shot and killed him. But we don't know if this was an accident or not. That's the part of the iceberg that Hemingway kept under water that empowered what he deemed to be his favorite story.

Hemingway's way to the unfathomable and divine was his own creative life, because through the redemptive power of writing he tapped into "the secret way of life." That's why he was driven to write; he had to nourish his life-hungry soul with the "juice" that he tapped into with every story that he wrote. That's the mystical nature of the creative process that I discovered through my own writing.

As he wrote, Hemingway inseminated the consciousness of his life experience with the magical ingredient of his imagination, which he compared to the dust of a butterfly's wings, thereby reconciling the opposing forces of his *enantiodromiac* nature. He reconciled his unconscious *shadow* energy with his conscious personality through the inherently self-transcending process of creative writing; but his *shadow* self was much too large for the great writer to reconcile, and it took over his life.

That's what I intuited while watching the movie *Hemingway and Gellhorn* over my ham and perogy dinner; I saw that Hemingway needed the powerful psychic energy of his *shadow* self to grow into the great writer that he was meant to be, because writing was his way of integrating his unconscious *shadow* with his conscious personality; and by the time the movie ended I had a new respect for my high school hero and literary mentor that I had grown to hate as a man.

When *Hemingway and Gellhorn* ended I no longer hated the man and loved the writer; I loved and admired both the cruel self-serving egoist given to pathological lying and the impeccable artist who was true to life in every story that he wrote, because they were two sides of the same paradoxical coin, which gave me a fresh perspective on my fellow man because once I saw how the *enantiodromiac* process worked in Hemingway's life I realized that this was "the secret way of life" that Jung had distilled into this psychology of individuation. Hemingway had to be a prick to become the great writer that he became; and that no longer bothered me.

6. The Hemingway Curse

There's a little Mr. Hyde in all of us, and in some of us it's not so little; it can be big enough to work its way out and take over our personality, like it did in Robert Louis Stevenson's novel *The Strange Case of Dr. Jekyll and Mr. Hyde,* and in real life it came out and took over Hemingway's personality late in his life; which was why he had to undergo electroshock treatment at the Mayo Clinic. But the treatment didn't work, and shortly after his last bout of treatment he took his own life.

Although Carl Jung put me wise to the Mr. Hyde side of our personality (what a great name Stevenson chose for our unconscious *shadow*), it was Gurdjieff who alerted me to what he called our "false personality." Not that I didn't know that I had a false personality, I had become aware of my false self in grade ten when I began to experience those strange impulses to falseness; but it was Gurdjieff who taught me how to harness the psychic energy of my false personality to "create" my own soul with the transformative power of his remarkable teaching.

The premise of Gurdjieff's teaching was that not everyone is born with an immortal soul, and to create our own soul we have to live a certain kind of life, which he attempted to provide at his *Institute for The Harmonious Development of Man* in Fontainebleau-Avon; this was why Gurdjieff attracted so many writers and artists who have always been concerned with matters of the soul but who puzzled the Parisian intelligentsia because they thought they were all crazy at the Institute.

I didn't know whether Gurdjieff was right or wrong in his belief that not everyone is born with an immortal soul, but that didn't matter to me. I knew that his teaching was my salvation, and I had to live it to make it work; which I did from the day I left university to forge my own path through life.

What pulled me into Gurdjieff's teaching was his belief that we don't have one central "I" but a multiplicity of separate little "Is" that can take over our personality anytime depending upon our mood and circumstance but which can be integrated into one harmonious single "I" by "working on oneself" with a teaching that he put together from many secret teachings that he studied in his twenty-year search for the meaning and purpose of life; a teaching which over time I came to see was nothing more nor less than the secret way of life that Jesus simply called the Way and in a conversation with Miguel Serrano in his book *C. G. Jung and Herman Hesse, A Record of Two Friendships* Carl Jung called "the path," and which he also told his young visitor Miguel Serrano was "very difficult."

That was why I fell in love with Jung, because he had found the secret way of life and lived it; but I did not become cognizant of this fact until I read Jung's quest for his lost soul in *The Red Book*. I had found the secret way of life also with Gurdjieff's teaching (which awakened me to the omnipresence of the Way that I came to call the omniscient guiding force of life), but I always felt that there was a subtext to all of Jung's writing, especially in his *Memories, Dreams, Reflections* and *The Undiscovered Self.* And when I read *The Red Book,* which was published fifty years after his death, I saw that the subtext of all his writing spoke to the secret way of life that he could not spell out openly because he wanted to keep the mystical nature of the gnostic experiences of life out of his psychology to safeguard the scientific credibility of his discipline; and suddenly I had a whole new respect for the man whom I believe today March 10, 2014 is still years ahead of his time.

Mr. Hyde then is our *shadow* personality, the dark repressed side of our conscious ego-personality, and what Jesus in *The Red Book* referred to as "the worm" which according to Jung's spiritual guide Philemon brings us "lamentation and abomination." But what I didn't know until I read Jung was that we also have a family *shadow*, a religion *shadow*, a workplace *shadow*, a community *shadow*, and a national *shadow*, and that the collective *shadow* personalities of the world constitute what Jung called the *Archetypal Shadow*, which he identified as the Devil; this is why in the Bible Satan proudly boasts that his name is legion.

So, there it was; the little devil in me came out that infamous night and took over my ego-personality and I had a sexual experience that so brutally shocked my conscience that I could not live with myself for shame and guilt and fled to France to find out why I did what I did because I knew that the "I" who had that sexual experience was not the real me; that's why I went on my quest for my true self.

I knew that the real me was lost somewhere deep inside my unconscious, but I had no guide like Philemon to show me the way; and I went out into the world to begin my quest for my true self. I had to forge my own way, which I did one painful experience at a time; and then I found my mentor in the pages of Ouspensky's book and whom I met in a dream one night shortly after I left university to live Gurdjieff's teaching in the real world outside the mental world of academia.

Gurdjieff was unbelievably magnetic in my dream, with large dark eyes awake and full of knowing, a handlebar moustache and shiny bald dome, and as intimidated as I was I had to know if he would accept me into his inner circle; but he told me that I wasn't ready yet, and I woke up from my dream feeling disappointed.

Two years later I dreamt of Gurdjieff again, and by this time I had made myself ready living his teaching. Gurdjieff and I were surrounded by a circle of his closest students. I was kneeling and he was standing. He placed his hands upon my shoulders and accepted me into his inner circle, and I was so happy I cried.

Dreams have always been a big part of my life. I met Carl Jung in a dream the year after I had seven past-life regressions and long after I had moved on from Gurdjieff's teaching. I was working on my "Soul talk" books (books that I talked into my mini recorder as I commuted to and from work every day), and although none of these books were transcribed let alone published, Jung came to me in my dream with my first volume *The Way of Soul* in his hand that he had to talk to me about because he was taken by my personal process of individuation that I referred to in my book as "the way of Soul." I had resolved the question that haunted Jung all of his life and which continued to haunt him on the other side, the question that he referred to as "the alpha and omega of the self," and we talked as long as his famous talk with Sigmund Freud upon their first meeting at Freud's home in Vienna, and I woke up from my dream bursting with irrepressible excitement.

My hero looked a bit younger than he did on the cover of his book *Memories, Dreams, Reflections*, a venerable and wise octogenarian still bursting with curiosity; and as we talked he would lean in to listen more closely, pipe in hand and piercing small eyes twinkling, and I would lean in to get as close as I could to soak up all the Jungian energy and gnostic wisdom that I could, but what I loved more than anything about my hero was his incredible sense of humor and soul-inspiring laughter.

That was five years ago, and I have not transcribed *The Way of Soul* from my tapes yet; and I have no idea if it will ever be published. But obviously on the other side it was published, because Jung had it in his hands when he came to me in my dream to discuss the secret way of life that I called "the way of Soul," and the day after my dream I began writing my novel *The Waking Dream* in which Jung played a central role; but as of today, March 11, 2014 it's still not published.

Dreams serve many functions, and one function of the dream is to be a gateway to the other side; and the irony of our conversation in my dream did not escape Jung. He rather enjoyed my banter about talking to him in my dream, because we were both cognizant of the fact that we were on the other side and that he was as real over there as he was before he died; and once we had a good laugh, we talked in earnest about the alpha and omega of the self and *The Way of Soul*.

So what happened to me in grade ten that changed my personality and affected my behavior with everyone I knew and met? What compelled my hero Hemingway in his youth to affect a persona that was not what he was but pretended to be?

Starting in school, Hemingway loved to boast and lie and pretend to be more than what he was, like creating the phoney gun club that he wrote about in the school paper; and although his bluster and bravado served him well in his sincere desire to become a writer—he loved to box, and he was always shadow boxing with great writers like Tolstoy and Dostoevsky or whichever writer he loved but felt threatened by—it fed his *shadow* personality with the psychic energy of his projections; but what separated him from other writers was his genuine desire to become a great writer, and he pursued his lofty goal with ferocious tenacity.

It was like he projected an image of himself onto the screen of his mind of what he wanted to be, and then he chased his image with unflagging tenacity until he caught up to himself; and he repeated the process year after year and wife after wife until he won what he sarcastically referred to as "the little Swedish thing"—a false hubristic modesty that characterized the great writer's deeply resentful nature from the moment he was awarded the prize that he coveted ever since his bitter rival William Faulkner was awarded the Nobel in 1949, five years before him.

But by the time Hemingway won the Nobel Prize his Mr. Hyde had become so selfish, dark, and menacing that he could no longer keep it down; and it burst through the defences of his mind and clouded his soul with dark bouts of "black-ass" depression that threatened his sanity with paranoid delusion of persecution that scared everyone who loved and knew him. That's why his wife Mary had him taken to the Mayo Clinic where he was treated with shock therapy; but it was too late. His Mr. Hyde was out to stay, and Hemingway felt compelled to shoot himself.

I have no doubt that's what happened to my literary mentor, and I cried when I got a look into his private hell in Hotchner's revealing memoir *Papa Hemingway*. My own father was also so *shadow*-afflicted that he had to have shock therapy. My father called it *"la schuola,"* and when he came home after treatment he was so terrified of *"la schuola"* that he quit drinking for three years; but his alcoholic demons came back and fueled his *shadow* personality with new energy, and when he found out that he had to go back to *"la schuola"* he had a stroke and landed in the hospital where he stayed comatose until he died a month later.

"You can't run away from crazy," said Mariel Hemingway, the movie star and great writer's granddaughter whose iconic fashion model sister Margaux graced the cover of *Time* but also committed suicide. Aside from Hemingway and his father, the great writer's brother and sister also took their own life, and though it wasn't on the record quite possibly his gender-conflicted son Gregory also took his own life, if not wittingly, unwittingly; which only helped to confirm the "Hemingway curse."

Mariel called the curse "our family karma," having come to the realization that she could not run away from crazy; and she was doing all she could to resolve the Hemingway *shadow* that she inherited by transforming her life with healthy living and athletics and making a documentary film *Running from Crazy* that chronicled her life and family history of mental illness and suicide, which she had directed by Academy Award-winning director Barbara Kopple and shown at the Sundance Film Festival; but it was a struggle for the great writer's granddaughter. In a courageous You Tube interview for *Running from Crazy*, Mariel revealed how her *family shadow* popped out into the light of day:

"My mother and father drank wine every night, and they called it "wine time" — always my favorite. And wine time started about 5:00, and my mother would sit on the countertop in the kitchen, and her feet were like crossed in the sink—every night, same place. You know, they'd have one glass of wine, and things were kind of happy, and they were actually having a regular conversation. But after a couple glasses of wine and the alcohol kicked in, nastiness would happen, uncomfortable—I can't remember why it would start, but there would—*some switch would happen.* Somebody's thrown a bottle against the wall, somebody gets cut. My mother would storm off to her bedroom, and my dad would go down into the basement, where he lived in his land of seclusion. And I would clean up the dinner party, the blood, the glass. It's just a—just weird, like it was the most normal thing to do, like that's what you did..."

I cannot count the number of times that I witnessed that same "switch" happening at home that Mariel witnessed when her family had "wine time" and seeing my *family shadow* pop out whenever my parents got into another one of their vicious arguments that always started over what seemed like nothing, with my mother always ending up calling my father one or all of her nasty soul-destroying jibes—"*disgraziato, mensognero,* and *vagabondo,*" which in plain English mean "you miserable bastard," "you barefaced liar," and "you lazy bum," and which always drove my father to the cantina in the basement to drink more wine and/or hard liquor because he was not man enough to drink his booze out in the open.

It was a vicious cycle, which Mariel Hemingway lived through in her family home and which she tried to break by not repeating the same soul-destroying life; and I went so far out of my way to break the back of our family beast with Gurdjieff's teaching of "work on oneself" that my mother said to me one day, "You change before my eyes. I don't know who you are anymore."

I was changing because I was becoming my true self, the self that my *family shadow* had overshadowed in grade ten when it melded with my ego-personality and cursed me with the archetypal *shadow* impulse to be false at every given opportunity; I was changing because I was becoming my true self.

7. The Mystic Marriage

In the *Gnostic Gospel of Thomas*, the disciples asked Jesus when the kingdom would come, and Jesus replied: *"When the two become one, and the outer like the inner, and the male with the female neither male nor female."*

Carl Jung, following the Gnostics, called this union of the outer with the inner a mystic marriage, or in Latin, *"mysterium coniunctionis,"* and his psychology was all about man's journey to the wholeness of this mystical union, which he called individuation; but Jung didn't provide a methodology as such for precipitating the process of individuation; that's why Gurdjieff was pulled into my life.

His teaching of "work on oneself" made the two into one; and so did Christ's teaching, but only if one lived it. This is what Jesus meant when he said to his disciples in Matthew's Gospel 7: 24: *"Whosoever heareth these sayings of mine, and doeth them, I will liken him unto a wise man, which built his house upon a rock."*

"Rock" is Christ's metaphor for the mystical union of the outer and inner self into one harmoniously integrated higher self which can only be realized through the process of individuation that is activated as one lives the sayings of Jesus, like doing charity work and not boasting about it. *"Take heed that ye do not your alms before men, to be seen of them,"* said Jesus in Matthew 6:1-3; *"otherwise you have no reward of your Father which is in heaven. But when thou doest alms let not thy left hand know what thy right hand doeth."*

Christ's teaching, Gurdjieff's teaching, or whatever name the secret way of life has manifested throughout history—be it through Gnosticism, Sufism, Taoism, the Socratic life of virtue, or whatever—it is always about the Way, which I came to recognize as the creative energy of life that is also known as *élan vital,* Logos, Spirit, the Word, Chi, Tao, Prana, Baraka and what I now identify as the omniscient guiding force of life and my literary mentor Hemingway naively called "juice."

Hemingway's granddaughter feared the "Hemingway curse," which she called her family karma, and she sought therapeutic counsel to ward off the mental illness that afflicted her family. Mariel poured her energy into holistic living because she no longer wanted to run away from crazy, something that her sister Margaux failed to do. Unlike her grandfather whose romantic lifestyle she tried to emulate with drink and drugs, Margaux didn't have a creative outlet to sublimate the psychic energies of her *shadow* self; and the self-destructive pattern of her *family shadow* took over her ego-personality and she killed herself. That was her family curse.

Her younger sister Mariel knew that. That's why she went the other way. She knew that her grandfather had an outlet for his creative energies, which he poured into the stories and novels that he wrote; and to save herself from her family curse Mariel poured her *shadow* energies into a balancing holistic lifestyle. And although I was not cognizant of this fact when I put Gurdjieff's teaching to practice in my life, like Mariel Hemingway I also had an intuitive feeling that I had to live a different kind of life to save myself from my own *shadow* and family curse.

As Jesus tells us, it's all a question of energy; do we build our house upon a rock or upon sand? Do we make the two into one and "create" our own soul, as Gurdjieff believed? Or do we feed our *shadow* self by squandering our creative energies like the great writer's granddaughter who finally lost control of her life to her family curse and ended up committing suicide like her grandfather?

We can no more run away from our family karma than we can deny our biology, and Mariel Hemingway got it right; but she couldn't quite grasp the mystery of the secret way of life, because if she had her journey to wholeness would not still be fraught with so much doubt. That's what Gurdjieff's teaching spared me.

Gurdjieff's teaching was a road map to my true self, but it was such a difficult teaching to live that many of his students became disillusioned, with some even committing suicide as Louis Pauwels tells us in his book *Gurdjieff*. But I was driven to find my true self, and I took Gurdjieff's teaching to the end: I did make the two into one and "created" my own soul, and I broke my family curse.

What then is this mystical union that Jung devoted his whole life trying to understand? He called the final work of his life-long study of the process of individuation *Mysterium Coniunctionis*, a massive tome that delves deeply into the alchemy of the mystical union of the outer and inner self; but it's difficult if not impossible to understand, because the secret way of life cannot be grasped by the mind alone. It has to be lived to be understood. As Gurdjieff liked to say, "There is only self-initiation into the mysteries of life."

Which is why Jesus said that one has to live his sayings to build his house upon a rock, because the secret way of life will only reveal itself as one lives it, not by studying it. And this is the secret of the mystic marriage. As Jesus tells us in the *Gospel of Thomas*: *"Whoever finds the interpretation of these sayings will not taste death."* I found the interpretation, and I no longer fear death.

Jean-Paul Sartre, whose existentialism I discovered in high school and later studied at university, was an atheist; and for him man did not have an immortal soul. Sartre saw man's existence as meaningless and absurd, and man was a useless passion condemned to be free, a purposeless process of *being* and *becoming*; and he summed up his philosophy with his paradoxical "I am what I am not, and I am not what I am" dilemma because he could not resolve the mystery of our inner and outer self—what he referred to in his philosophical tome

Being and Nothingness as the *being* and *non-being* aspects of our contingent and absurd existence.

I loved Sartre because of how seriously he took man's freedom and his magnificent effort to dignify man's absurd existence, and he gave me much to think about; but I believed in God, and I knew in that deep intuitive way that our life was not contingent and absurd. There was meaning and purpose to life, and all I had to do was find it; that's why I never stopped seeking, even after I discovered Gurdjieff's road map of the soul and resolved the paradox of my inner and outer self, and—oh irony!—all of my years of questing for my true self brought me right back to creative writing and my high school hero!

Ernest Hemingway's life was a paradox. He was both his false *shadow* self and his impeccably true writer self who began every story that he wrote with one true sentence, as he tells us in his memoir *A Moveable Feast*; and the tragedy of his life was that despite his devotion to the inherently self-transcending process of creative writing, he was never able to resolve the paradox of the conflicted nature of his *being* and *non-being*; and not until I watched the movie *Hemingway and Gellhorn* did I appreciate that like the philosopher of existentialism my high school hero had also trapped himself in the conundrum of his own becoming.

Hemingway's curse was that he could not resolve his *shadow* and transcend himself, despite the disciplined routine of his daily writing. As his granddaughter so wisely expressed it, he could not run away from crazy because wherever he went his unresolved *shadow* would be there to haunt him; and it didn't help that Hemingway loved to drink wine and hard liquor every day, because alcohol turned on that psychic "switch" that set his *shadow* free to take over his massive ego-personality, and then all hell would break loose and the great author became very nasty.

Hemingway's mental illness was his unresolved *shadow* self, and no pharmaceuticals or therapy—psychotherapeutic or shock treatment—can soothe the wild beast of the *shadow* side of our personality; all that does is repress the *shadow* back to the unconscious where it broods and waits for the next "switch" to set it free, like alcohol or an innocent comment that touches a raw nerve.

That's what Gurdjieff taught me. And my father too. I watched my father's life break down as he gave way to his disturbing *shadow*, but I was helpless to do anything about it. I tried to help my father overcome our family curse, but I failed because karma is an individual responsibility; and my father was not wise enough to integrate his *shadow* and transcend himself. Like all good Italian Roman Catholics who lean upon their faith for salvation, my father prayed to Jesus to protect him from the Devil, little realizing that he was the author of his own misery; and it didn't matter how many candles he lit to invoke help from Jesus and the Holy Saints, my father was cursed by the demons of his own conflicted *shadow* self.

That's the tragedy of the family curse, and the best gift that parents can give to their children is a *shadow* that's not so conflicted; because the more resolved one's *family shadow* is, the easier life will be for the children and grandchildren because they won't have a "big bag" to drag behind them, as Robert Bly poetically referred to our *shadow* in his brilliant essay "The Long Bag We Drag Behind Us" in the book of essays *Meeting the Shadow, The Hidden Power of the Dark Side of Human Nature,* by Connie Zweig and Jeremiah Abrams.

The Hemingway *family shadow* was dangerously conflicted, which could be seen in Ernest's own bipolar father whose behavior could switch from loving father one moment to "strict disciplinarian" the next who strapped his children for going against his will, such as dancing which he did not allow because it was evil, and it severely handicapped the children and grandchildren; like the androgynous great writer's third son who was so gender-conflicted that he went through life tormented by his own unresolved sexuality that eventually compelled him to have a sex change operation, as his wife Valerie Hemingway tells us in her courageous memoir *Running with the Bulls, My Years with the Hemingways.* Her husband Gregory "Gigi" Hemingway had a very sad and tortured life.

Gregory's father had a lot of issues, which he brilliantly worked into his short stories and novels; but, as Katherine Mansfield realized so young in life, despite the fact that Hemingway called her stories near-beer, literature is not enough; and one has to find a way to resolve the fundamental issue of our *enantiodromiac* nature.

That's why I had to become a seeker instead of a writer; I had to resolve the disturbing nature of my *shadow* self that was set free that godforsaken night (now, in retrospect, it was not godforsaken after all; but the most propitious night of my entire life because it catapulted me into my quest for my true self) and compelled me to have a sexual experience that shocked my conscience awake, and out of shame and guilt I spent my best and most creative energies looking for my true self; and only after I found my true self could I dedicate my life to writing.

It was ironic then that I became a seeker first and not a writer, because in my quest for my true self I learned that literature would not have been enough to satisfy my longing for wholeness and singleness of self. I had to find the secret way of life to find my true self, and when I found Gurdjieff's teaching the natural process of individuation opened up to me with every experience that I had, because now I had "eyes" to see and "ears" to hear, and the Way led me to my true self.

8. Getting Ready for Hemingway

Literature may not be enough to satisfy the longing in our soul, but it is one of the most satisfying ways to nourish our spiritual hunger; which is why writers write and readers can't get enough of their stories. But what is the power of story?

Once again, my mentor came to my aid, as always happens whenever the target draws forth the arrow. Jung first came to offer me a psychological perspective on evil and liberated me from my inflexible Christian faith with his book *Answer to Job*; and he came to me again to expand my perspective on my false personality with his psychological essays in *Aion*; and this time he came to me by way of Laurens van der Post's book *Jung and the Story of Our Time* which introduced me to the mythic power of story that helped me see what Jung called the "transcendent function" of Hemingway's creative genius.

Hemingway's creative genius was his gift for writing stories. Every writer has this gift to some degree; but Hemingway had it full measure, and had not Jung introduced me to the mythic power of story—and by this I mean the power of story to convey the secret truth of life—I would never have seen Hemingway's creative genius that made Hemingway the great writer that he became.

The secret truth of life nourishes our spiritual hunger; that's why we love to read stories—and poetry, of course; because poetry offers us such tasty morsels of truth that we can snack on them to our heart's contentment. But stories are full course meals, and novels can be banquets of life-truth, as Hemingway's novels were, like his sweetly satisfying novel *The Old Man and the Sea*. But what is this secret truth of life that writers give to the world with their creative genius?

When I connected the dots and realized that the *élan vital*, Logos, Spirit, the Word, Chi, Baraka, Prana, "juice," and the omniscient guiding force of life were all one and the same expression of the ground of all being which is *Consciousness*, the puzzle of life began to make sense to me; and all divisions between people, paths, politics, religions, and philosophies disappeared, and this brought me to the simple realization that life itself is the way—which was the same conclusion C. G. Jung had come to in *The Red Book*. "This life is the way, the long sought-after way to the unfathomable, which we call divine. There is no other way, all other ways are false paths," he wrote; making each person's story a carrier of the truth of life.

This is the power of story. Each and every person has their own story, and their story carries the secret truth of life. And because no two people are the same, each person's story carries its own truth. This is the secret power of story that writers seek with every story they write and why readers love to read stories.

In his book *Jung and the Story of Our Time*, Laurens van der Post tells Jung a personal story of his relationship with the Bushmen, the first people of South Africa, of how reluctant they were to tell their stories to strangers for fear that they would not be respected; which was why they remained a secret to outsiders.

"I realized that the story was their most precious possession and they were protecting it the best way they could," wrote Laurens van der Post; and he went on to explain to Jung that story was the seed and essence of the Bushmen's history, the carrier of their people's collective truth that guided them through life, and only when one had earned the privilege would he be told their stories.

Laurens van der Post earned this privilege with an old Bushman grandmother, and he got to hear some of the first people of South Africa's stories; which excited Jung very much, because while working at the Burgholzli psychiatric hospital in Zurich he made the most fascinating discovery of his career when he realized that the reason his patients were in the mental hospital was because their personal story had been interrupted—by the death of a child or loved one, the loss of a job, a personal betrayal, or whatever traumatic misfortune that befell them; and Jung realized that to heal his patients he had to re-connect them with their life story.

Their life story was their most precious possession whether they realized it or not, Jung told his new friend Laurens van der Post on their first meeting where they talked for five hours in the warmth of a cozy fire at Jung's home; and if a person's story got interrupted they fell apart. That was the insight that opened a window on man's soul for Jung, and he learned to respect every person's story because it was their truth and way to the unfathomable and divine.

My heart leapt with joy when I read this, because it confirmed my own understanding of the secret power of story; but my window on man's soul had been opened to karma and reincarnation, which added a whole new dimension of truth to every person's story because it explained something about the soul's code that Jung could not write about for fear of damaging his scientific credibility.

Like my literary mentor who kept to the existential dimension of life, so too did Jung stick to the one-life theory to preserve his scientific integrity; but near the end of his life he did admit to the possibility of reincarnation. "The question of karma is obscure to me, as is also the problem of personal rebirth or the transmigration of souls," he wrote. "Recently, however, I observed in myself a series of dreams which would seem to describe the process of reincarnation in a deceased person of my acquaintance. I must confess, however, that after this experience I view the problem of reincarnation with somewhat different eyes, though without being in a position to assert a definite opinion" (*Memories, Dreams, Reflections*, p. 319).

I never doubted that reincarnation was a fact of life given my past-life recollection dreams in my teens, which helped me to accept what Socrates revealed in Plato's *Phaedo*: "There is a doctrine uttered in secret that man is a prisoner who has no right to open the door of his prison and run away; this is a great mystery which I do not quite understand," but after years of reading and seven past-life regressions, I could see that Socrates was being coy when he said that he did not quite understand this mystery, because the *transcendent function* of his philosophy was all about liberating soul from the prison of our body through a life of virtue, of which he made Goodness the most noble and I made central to my personal ethic; so I had a wider perspective on the soul's code than my mentor, which was probably why he came to me in my dream to talk about my book *The Way of Soul.*

From my own past-life regressions I traced the karmic history of some of my most extreme lifetimes, like my morally and sexually depraved lifetime as the *"le salaud de Paris"* (scoundrel of Paris) that had to be brought into karmic balance beginning with my next incarnation as a black slave in southern Georgia known to my people as "Solomon the Good," and how my relationship with Penny, the love of my current lifetime, came about because I had abandoned her for my mistress when she was my wife in our past lifetime together in Genoa, Italy; and along with the karmic connections I made with some of my other past lives, I could no longer deny that we all have a karmic destiny that is distinct but necessary for our soul's code to realize our wholeness and singleness of self.

Our life story then is our karmic destiny, which HAS to play itself out; and if it is interrupted by whatever circumstance we will just keep coming back until we get it right and bring closure to our life story. Because we have free will, we can deter our karmic destiny by veering off in another direction; but we will only be dragged back by our spiritual destiny (our soul's code), and this only makes for a very difficult life—as I have experienced in my current lifetime.

I resisted bringing my life story to closure, and my *daemon* compelled me to write my poem "Noman" in grade twelve that opened up my consciousness to the *shadow personality* of my morally and sexually depraved past life as *"le salaud de Paris"* which possessed me the night I had that sexual experience that shocked my conscience awake and catapulted me into my quest for my true self, thereby confirming the wisdom of Cleanthes' poem that we can be led by our destiny or dragged by it; that's why I took to Gurdjieff's teaching, because by "working" on myself I precipitated the *transcendent function* of my self-becoming.

The *transcendent function* is the key to Jung's psychology, because only through a process of engaging the *transcendent function* can a person hasten the psychological growth that leads to individuation; and by *transcendent function* Jung meant the union of the conscious and unconscious content of the self.

"The *transcendent function* is the means by which the unity or self archetype is realized," said Jung in his essay "The Transcendent Function." In effect then, Gurdjieff's teaching provided me with the *transcendent function* that I needed to integrate the many little "Is" of my self-consciousness and individuate them into one single "I", or what Jesus referred to as making the inner and outer self into one; and in doing so I resolved the *enantiodromiac* paradox of my *being* and *non-being* and gave birth to my spiritual self, just as Jesus promised if one lived his teaching.

"The *transcendent function* is endowed with the capability of uniting all of the opposing trends in the personality and of working toward the goal of wholeness," said Jung in his essay; and that's precisely what I did by "working" on myself, which I expressed in my journal when I finally achieved my goal: *"I am what I am not, and I am not what I am; I am both, but neither: I am Soul."*

I transcended myself and realized my wholeness, and I remember the exact moment when it happened. I was standing in the doorway of my mother's kitchen. She was kneading bread dough on the kitchen table. We were talking. Suddenly a feeling came over me and I knew that I was immortal. But it was more than just a feeling. It was a certainty that possessed all of me. In that one eternal moment of spiritual self-realization consciousness, I knew that I was immortal and would never die.

After all my years of questing and "working" on myself I had finally found my true self, and I never felt such relief in my entire life. It felt like the burden of the world had been lifted off my shoulders, and I was free to be myself.

If there could be one moment when the acorn seed could realize that it has finally become an oak tree, that would be the same kind of realization that I experienced as the feeling of my own immortality came over me as my mother kneaded bread dough on the kitchen table; and from that moment on I have never doubted my immorality. And although I did not realize it until many years later, I had just outgrown my mentor Gurdjieff; which was why the divine law of synchronicity once again came into play in my life by providing me with the opportunity a few days later (perhaps a week or two, I can't quite remember when) to embrace a new teaching better suited to my new state of consciousness.

I embraced my new teaching and continued on my journey through life; but I no longer had to struggle to unite the opposing forces of my personality to become one united single self; I was whole, and the rest of my journey was to grow in my wholeness and singleness of self within the paradigm of my new teaching which I lived for many years before I outgrew it also and stepped into my own path.

The acorn had become an oak tree, and for over thirty years I grew in my wholeness until I was ready for my own path which the merciful law of synchronicity once again provided me with in the movie *Hemingway and Gellhorn* that I *had* to watch because I felt that Hemingway was going to tell me something that would satisfy that unsatisfied longing in my soul to be the writer I could never become because I had to find my true self first; and that's the back story of how I came back to Hemingway to become the writer I always wanted to be.

9. On the Edge of a Precipice

Some people are born to be who they are meant to be, and they step into their destiny as soon as they find their point of entry—like going to medical school, starting your own band to satisfy you're musical calling, or getting a job with the *Kansas City Star* like Hemingway did to answer his own call to writing.

I envied Hemingway in my youth, and most of my life really because he did not have to run the race just to get to the starting line; he was born to be the person he was meant to be. I had to *become* the person I was meant to be; only then could I satisfy the longing in my soul to be a writer like my high school hero.

I could not become the person I was meant to be by becoming a writer, because my *daemon* knew that literature would not be enough to bring closure to my karmic destiny; so I had to find the *transcendent function* best suited for my individuation, which came to me by way of Gurdjieff's teaching.

I've told this story in my fiction, because only through fiction could I be true to my life story; and now that I've brought closure to my karmic destiny I have embraced my new path and devoted the rest of my life to becoming the writer I always wanted to be. And I began to live my new path shortly after I saw the movie *Hemingway and Gellhorn* by applying everything that I had learned about creative writing to my new book of stories whose working title was "I Am, and Life is Merely Something that I Do" but which after writing the first few stories evolved into the much more intriguing reader-catchy title *Enantiodromia*.

I've always loved writing, but since my return to Hemingway it terrifies me. I can't explain why, but writing has taken on a whole new meaning that I've never experienced before. It feels like I'm standing on the edge of a precipice, and I'm terrified of falling off. But I know I have to jump, because that's what it means to be the writer I've always wanted to be; which reminds me of what my mentor said in his acceptance speech when he received the Nobel Prize for Literature:

"For a true writer each book should be a new beginning where he tries again for something that is beyond attainment. He should always try for something that has never been done or that others have tried and failed. Then sometimes, with great luck, he will succeed.

"How simply the writing of literature would be if it were only necessary to write in another way what has been well written. It is because we have had such great writers in the past that a writer is driven far out past where he can go, out to where no one can help him."

That's exactly how I felt when I came back to Hemingway with my new book of short stories; like I had been driven far out past where I can go, out to where no one can help me; and, believe me, it's a terrifying place to be because one stands alone with his conscience. Which brings to mind something that I wrote way back then in Annecy one night after I came in from the loneliest walk of my life; something that came to me from the deepest depths of my soul that was to inspire every step of the way in my long and painful journey to my true self:

"Steadfast and courageous is he, who having overcome woe and grief remains alone and undaunted. Alone I say, for to be otherwise would hardly seem possible; for one must bear one's conscience alone. He must fight the battle and he must win the battle, odds or not odds. He must win to establish the equilibrial tranquility of body and soul, and sooner or later he will erupt as a volcano of unlimited confidence which will purpose his life thereafter. And having given birth to such magnificence he will no

longer be alone alone, but alone in society; and he will see the mirror of his puerile grief in the eyes of his fellow man."

Having found my true self, that's exactly the way I feel today, alone in society; but what a journey it's been from the night I wrote that in Annecy, France in 1968 to my life today in 2014 in Georgian Bay, Ontario. Carl Gustav Jung is the only person that I have read (and met in my dream) aside from Gurdjieff who achieved wholeness and singleness of self, which is why I have unparalleled respect for him; but after watching *Hemingway and Gellhorn* I had an unexpected shift in my personal paradigm that filled me with new respect for the writer that I had grown to hate for the self-centered egoist that he had become.

This was a strange experience for me, and I can only explain it by way of another strange but similar experience that I had after reading the chronicle of Jung's quest for his lost soul, *Liber Novus*, better known as *The Red Book*.

After reading *The Red Book*, the puzzle that I always felt Carl Jung's life to be suddenly made sense to me. It was like *The Red Book* was the missing piece to the puzzle of Carl Jung's life, and it unlocked the mystery of all his writing; that's how the movie *Hemingway and Gellhorn* affected me, because in some artistic way it unlocked the mystery of Hemingway's paradoxical personality.

I couldn't explain it, just as I couldn't explain my newfound consciousness on Jung's writing after reading *The Red Book*; which was why I HAD to go back to Hemingway after watching *Hemingway and Gellhorn*. I felt compelled to re-read everything Hemingway that I had in my library and order from Amazon all the Hemingway literature that I felt strongly nudged to read—*The Complete Short Stories of Ernest Hemingway*, which I didn't have; *The Hemingway Women*, by Bernice Kert; *Paris without End: The True Story of Hemingway's First Wife*, by Gioia Diliberto; *Hemingway: The Final Years*, by Michael Reynolds; and two of Hemingway's books that I did not have: *The Torrents of*

Spring and *Men without Women*; and I also ordered *The Selected Letters of C. G. Jung, 1909-1961* because I had to have a new Jung fix to satisfy my need to know Jung's private thoughts.

I had no idea why I was inspired to pair these two great men the way I have in this memoir; but I've learned to trust my creative instinct, and I knew that somewhere in the process I would be told the reason why, and now I know.

My high school hero and literary mentor Ernest Hemingway and my quest-for-my-true self hero Carl Gustav Jung stand at the opposite ends of the spectrum: Hemingway could not resolve the paradoxical dilemma of his individuation process by employing the *transcendent function* of creative writing to integrate his false *shadow* self with his personality, and Jung resolved the paradox of his superior and self-serving *shadow* self with his personality by going on a quest for his lost soul.

Hemingway and Jung were polar opposites. It was like they symbolized the Yin and Yang of life; *enantiodromiac* opposites, with Hemingway growing more into his *shadow* personality as he grew older, and Jung growing out of his *shadow* personality as he grew older, as though the two men represented everything there was to know about the *enantiodromiac* process of human nature.

That's why my Muse brought them together, because they both reflected my life in separate ways; and it was my job to bring clarity to the mind-boggling mystery of the *enantiodromiac* process that lies at the heart of life, and literature.

10. The Hemingway Effect

When I first read Hemingway in high school I enjoyed how clean and simple his writing was; I had absolutely no idea that he was writing that way for effect, a style that he worked on laboriously and which he later elaborated on by explaining his "iceberg theory," which he said he learned from Cezanne and called it his "secret" that would give his writing the impact of Cezanne's paintings.

In *A Moveable Feast*, Hemingway's melancholy memoir of his apprenticeship days in Paris as a young man, he tells us that he often went to the Luxembourg Museum to study the great paintings (which have now been mostly transferred to the Louvre); he went nearly every day, he said, "for the Cezannes and to see the Manets and the Monets and other Impressionists...I was learning something from the paintings of Cezanne that made writing simple true sentences far from enough to make the stories have the dimensions that I was trying to put in them. I was learning very much from him but I was not articulate enough to explain it to anyone. Besides it was my secret" (*A Moveable Feast*, p. 13).

Later, when he was articulate enough to explain his "secret," he called it his "iceberg theory," which simply stated meant that he could leave out of his story the knowledge that could be implied in his story to give his story greater emotional impact; for example, in his short story "Out of Season," Hemingway tells us in his memoir that he had omitted the real end of the story, which was that the old man hanged himself. "This was omitted on my new theory that you could omit anything if you knew that you omitted and the omitted part would strengthen the story and make people feel something more than they understood" (Ibid., p. 75).

Once he realized how effective his "secret" was, he employed it to all of his stories; and when he got to write his novel that launched his career, *The Sun Also Rises*, it was his "secret" that gave his story the impact that puzzled readers until they learned the crucial bit of information that gave the story the emotional impact that he was trying to achieve and which in my estimation was his first real work on par with Cezanne's art—the knowledge that Jake Barnes, who was in love with Lady Bret Ashely, could not sexually consummate his love for her because he had a war wound that precluded having sexual intercourse.

Jake's war wound was implied in the story but never openly revealed. That's the part of the "iceberg" that was underwater which could not be seen; but it was there, in the story, just as the greater part of the iceberg that was underwater that gave the much smaller upper part of the iceberg all of its gravitas; which was exactly what Hemingway intended with Jake's war wound. Pure creative genius!

Hemingway's "secret" was the biggest part of what I've come to call "the Hemingway effect." The other factors that went into creating "the Hemingway effect" that has inspired generations of writers were his clean and simple (though simple is not the correct word) style, and his personal credo to "tell it the way it was," which according to Carlos Baker's *Hemingway: The Writer as Artist* involved mastering the three most essential factors of a good story: a sense of place, a sense of fact, and a sense of scene. And, of course, building his story on one true sentence which always gave his stories the quality of real beer.

To better understand Hemingway's clean and simple style (scholars have determined that Hemingway's writing vocabulary was limited to nine hundred words), he was once taunted by one of his fellow but rival writers, William Faulkner (who had won the Noble Prize for Literature in 1949, which naturally embittered the great competitive writer who finally won his Nobel in 1954), when he let it be known to the world that Hemingway was afraid to use big words. Hemingway responded to his young friend Hotchner, "Poor Faulkner. Does he really think big emotions come from big words? He thinks I don't know the ten-dollar words. I know them all right. But there are older and simpler and better words, and those are the ones I use" (*Papa Hemingway*, A. E. Hotchner, pp. 69-70).

Hemingway said he read the Bible right through every year because he loved the simple writing and wisdom of the Bible, which may have been true for a year or so but which I tend to believe was another one of his great exaggerations that added to the mythic stature to the writer; but his logic was sound: the Bible is an enduring chronicle, and the style of the writing had to be a critical factor for its endurance; so why not emulate the clean and simple style of the writers of the Bible?

Nonetheless, Hemingway explained how he arrived at his one true sentence principle in his memoir, his final word on writing: "But sometimes when I was starting a new story and I could not get it going, I would sit in front of the fire and squeeze the peel of the little oranges into the edge of the flame and watch the sputter of blue that they made. I would stand and look out over the roofs of Paris and think, 'Do not worry. You have always written before and you will write now. All you have to do is write one true sentence. Write the truest sentence that you know.'" And he went on to say, thereby confirming his real beer credo, "If I started to write elaborately, or like someone introducing or presenting something, I found that I could cut that scrollwork or ornament out and throw it away and start with the first true simple declarative sentence I had written. Up in that room I decided that I would write one story about each thing that I knew about" (*A Moveable Feast*, p. 12). That's how he arrived at his credo to "tell it the way it was."

Hemingway had another "secret" which he could not have articulated in his youth even if he could articulate it, because this second "secret" could only have been realized after a long life of seasoned writing, a "secret" that presupposes all the wisdom of the seeker who has found enlightenment.

To understand the profound depths of Hemingway's second literary "secret," it would be best to compare it to an ancient Buddhist saying: *Before enlightenment, you chop wood and carry water. After enlightenment, you chop wood and carry water.* Speaking about *The Old Man and the Sea,* in a letter to Bernard Berenson in 1952, Hemingway wrote: "Then there is the other secret. There isn't any symbolysm (mis-spelled). The sea is the sea. The old man is an old man. The boy is a boy and the fish is a fish. The shark are all sharks no better and no worse. All the symbolism that people say is shit. *What goes beyond is what you see beyond when you know.* A writer should know too much" (*Selected Letters,* p. 780, Italics mine).

This "secret" is so hermetically sealed that only one who has discovered it can understand it. This is one of those mysteries that Gurdjieff would say one has to be initiated into to understand; and the only way to initiate oneself into this mystery is by doing it—which in this case, means writing, and writing, and more writing.

I understood Hemingway's second and most inaccessible "secret" because I was a truth seeker first and a writer second, and I was fortunate enough to be one of the thirty birds (a reference to the Sufi allegory *A Conference of the Birds*) to complete my journey and find my true self; so, in all modesty, I possess the sacred knowledge that allows me to see what Hemingway meant by his second "secret," and which is simply this: Hemingway the acorn-seed writer had finally become Hemingway the oak-tree writer, and he spoke from the enlightened consciousness of his fully realized Hemingway writer self; and from this perspective, what he wrote in his stories was as it was and not a symbolic expression of what it pointed to; a description of things as they actually were in all their natural glory.

A symbol, as my other hero C. G. Jung tells us in *Man and his Symbols,* "implies something more than its obvious and immediate meaning. It has a wider 'unconscious' aspect that is never precisely defined or fully explained." This speaks to the guidance that comes from the secret way of life that one activates when he is fully engaged in his own *transcendent function*, as Hemingway was with his creative writing. But when one has realized his goal of becoming the oak tree of his becoming, which in this case means becoming an enlightened writer, then the symbols cease to be symbols and stand as they are in their true nature—after enlightenment you chop wood and carry water, as it were.

This is why Hemingway, who had no insight into how the omniscient guiding force of life worked (though he believed in its guidance by way of his superstitious belief in good and bad luck, which is why he always carried good luck charms in his pocket, like his lucky rabbit's foot), always scoffed when people talked about symbols in his writing—his greatest irritation coming from the symbol of the dried and frozen carcass of a leopard near the summit of Mount Kilimanjaro in his short story "The Snows of Kilimanjaro" which bared the soul of the great writer.

But by the time Hemingway wrote *The Old Man and the Sea* he had become the accomplished writer that he worked so hard to become, and he was simply telling a story about an old man and his fish—*imagining it so truly that it was as though it had actually happened.* That's the genius of "the Hemingway effect."

11. Hemingway's Sisyphean Struggle

"An acorn grows into a tree and not a donkey," said my mentor C. G. Jung; and so do we all grow into the person we are meant to be. This is what Jungian analyst James Hillman purported with his book *The Soul's Code*. But there's a hidden piece to this puzzle that Jung and Hillman could not explain, because it wasn't in their purview to do so; and that's my precipice, because I've solved the puzzle of life and hesitate to explain it for fear of poking the beast.

In a private letter to Anonymous dated November 1, 1951, Carl Jung explained to this person why it was so difficult to reveal the truth to people: "...in the end people don't want to know what secrets are slumbering in their souls. If you struggle too much to penetrate into another person, you find that you have thrust him into a defensive position, and resistance develops because, through your efforts to penetrate and understand, he is forced to examine those things in himself which he doesn't want to examine. Everybody has a dark side which—so long as all goes well—he had better not know about" (*Selected Letters of C. G. Jung, 1909-1961*).

At the risk of poking the beast, then; let me explain what I have uncovered. I have no doubt that we're all encoded with our own individual traits and are driven by the conatus of our soul's code to realize the wholeness and singleness of self of our own individuality just as the acorn is teleologically driven to become an oak tree and not a donkey, and that the purpose of life is to grow into the person we are meant to be; but because we have free will we can veer so far off our destined course that we can lose our way entirely and like Macbeth cry out that life is a tale told by an idiot full of sound and fury signifying nothing. That's our dilemma.

How do we stay on our destined course, then? And how do we even know that we have a destined course, because most people don't seem to be called to be the person they are meant to be? They live their life without the ambition that drives people of destiny, and it's not in them to understand a person of ambition like my heroes Hemingway and Jung; so what does it mean to be called?

Being a seeker first and writer second, I made it my mission to find out why I had to find my true self; so I know what it means to be called, and after working it out in novels like *Keeper of the Flame* and *Healing with Padre Pio*, the short answer is that we have two destinies: one karmic, which is totally determined by the choices we make in life; and the other spiritual, which is fixed by providential design but can only be realized through our karmic destiny. And our dilemma in life has always been to bring our karmic destiny into agreement with our spiritual destiny.

As the Stoic philosopher Cleanthes said, we can walk alongside our spiritual destiny or we can be dragged by it. If we walk alongside our spiritual destiny, we have aligned our two destines and are in sync with ourselves and life; but if we are dragged by our spiritual destiny, we are out of sync with ourselves and life, and we suffer the indignity of our own karmic blindness. Which is why I'm preoccupied with Hemingway and Jung who represent the two paths to our destined self.

Hemingway fought his spiritual destiny every step of the way by the selfish choices he made until he could fight with himself no longer and took his own life; and Jung worked with himself to find his lost soul and realized his true self, which led him late in life to say, "Thank God I'm Jung and not a Jungian" because it was the purpose of his psychology for every person to realize their own individuality through their own *transcendent function*, which Hemingway tried with all of his might to do through the inherently self-transcending function of his creative calling but failed to realize because his *shadow* had grown too large for him to integrate into his true self—a modern, but tragic hero not unlike the mythical Sisyphus whose own hubris condemned him to rolling a rock up a mountain for eternity.

"One must imagine Sisyphus happy," concluded Camus in his book of essays *The Myth of Sisyphus*; but I could not imagine Sisyphus happy. Like Camus, Hemingway found fulfillment in the struggle towards the summit, which he reflected in every story that he wrote and which appealed to his readers because his stories captured their own Sisyphean struggle with life that Hemingway mythologized in his most consummate work, *The Old Man and the Sea*; but as satisfying as Hemingway's stories may be to read, they leave one wanting something more.

Like his short story, "A Clean, Well-Lighted Place" that he wrote long before Camus attempted to solve the only true philosophical problem of suicide by imagining Sisyphus happy condemned to a fate of rolling a rock up a mountain whence it rolled back down of its own accord and rolling it back up again and again without end, and the lonely old man getting drunk every night in the clean well-lighted café who tried to commit suicide by hanging himself but was saved by his niece, and the older and younger waiters in the café, each person living out their own chosen path, and Hemingway ending his little story without resolution because he could not see the why of life that left one hollow for not knowing, but the story froze that eternal moment of *nada* that the lonely old man and older waiter who suffered from insomnia felt as Sisyphus descended from his summit leaving one wondering if life was worth the struggle that the philosopher philosophized was enough to fill a man's heart and which Hemingway tried to prove by living his life to the fullest every time he embraced his own fate with a new wife and new adventure but which never explained what that dried and frozen carcass of a leopard was seeking near the summit of the House of God, and one is left a little sadder and more conscious of life but no wiser; and real beer or not, Hemingway just wasn't enough to satisfy the longing in our soul for wholeness and singleness of self.

So what if he had pissed out more life than I had lived? What did it matter how much life he had pissed out when all the life that he lived added up to such a big fat *nada* that the crushing weight of his own nothingness forced him to shoot himself? If literature was not enough, then neither was life; that's why my *daemon* drove me to find my true self first. I had to find the meaning of my life.

I had many lives where I had gorged myself on life, especially my lifetime as *"le salaud de Paris"* in the mid-17th Century; so it wasn't my destiny to get the most out of life so I could write about it like my high school hero, because my destiny was more about how to live my life than how much life I lived so I could answer the question that came to me in another dream shortly after I dreamt of Hemingway.

In my dream I left my body and entered into the mind of every person in the world; and I took every question that every person in the world had ever asked and reduced them all to one simple question: WHY AM I? That's what compelled me to study philosophy at university when I returned to Canada; I had to find an answer to the question that haunted every single person in the world.

I came into this life to bring closure to the cycle of my karmic destiny, then; because unless we know why we keep coming back into life we will just keep coming back until we know why we are. So I could not devote my life to writing like my high school hero; I had to find my true self first, which I did; and when I saw the movie *Hemingway and Gellhorn* I heard the call to become the writer that I always wanted to be; and to do that I knew I had to go back to Hemingway, because of all the writers that I had read he was the one who still spoke to me.

Why am I? is not a question that people normally ask. The question that people normally ask is *who am I?* People ask this question because they have not yet realized their true self, and they crave to be the person they are meant to be.

Who am I? is our soul's cry for attention. When Jung cried out: "My soul, where are you?" he was asking himself, *who am I?* He had accomplished all of his No. 1 personality goals—"honor, power, wealth, knowledge, and every human happiness"—but it was not enough to satisfy his essential need to be the person he was meant to be; and he became possessed by an overpowering desire to tend to his No. 2 personality which he had neglected, thus beginning his "confrontation with the unconscious" to look for his lost soul in the depths of his own being.

But if *who am I?* addresses our soul's essential need to be the person we are meant to be, what Jung called his No. 2 personality, what does the question *why am I?* address if not what Jung called his No. 1 personality? In my dream, this question was asked by every person in the world; but what does this mean?

It took many years of "work" on myself to answer this question, both what it addressed and why every person has a need to know why they are; and the answer has to do with the *enantiodromiac* process that drives our soul through life, the *being* and *non-being* of our essential nature. Despite what Buddhists believe about man not having an autonomous individual self, maintaining that our ego self is illusory and non-real, my quest for my true self has proven that we do have an autonomous individual self; but we have to go through the natural process of individuation to realize our soul self, and the more we grow in our essential nature, the more we want to become the person we are meant to be. But we need energy to grow into our true self; much more energy than life can provide. And that's our dilemma.

Everything that lives must have energy to grow, and the essential energy of life is *élan vital*, which is the creative life force; and for us to grow into the person we are meant to be we have to have this life-giving energy, which we take in through the air we breathe, the food we eat, the liquids we drink, and the things we do. Very few people realize it, but doing takes in the vital life force too; and the more we do, the more life force we take in and grow into the person we are meant to be, and how much we do depends upon our need to be the person we are meant to be.

In the doing, we experience life; so the more life we experience, the more vital life force we take in to nourish our essential need for self-identity. Like the acorn's need to be an oak tree, so do we all have an essential need to be the person we are meant to be; and my high school hero had a voracious need to be a great writer, and he fed his voracious need by experiencing all the life that he could live—both small and big game hunting, trout and deep-sea fishing, travelling, boxing, bullfighting, eating, drinking, and having sex; to name only the major interests of his life. That's how he fed his enormous appetite to become the great writer he wanted to be.

When he was asked by George Plimpton for the *Paris Review* if he could recall the exact moment when he decided to become a writer, he replied: "No, I always wanted to be a writer." This was his karmic destiny, and he was going to be a great writer no matter what; that's what drove my high school hero to be so selfish in his desire to satisfy his need to be the best writer of his generation and achieve literary immortality. "There is no use writing anything that has been written before unless you can beat it," he wrote in a piece for *Esquire* in 1935; that's why he shadow-boxed with the great writers with every novel that he wrote.

Not everyone is driven to satisfy their need to be the person they are meant to be; only people who crave to be what they are meant to be. But where does this craving come from? Why do some people have it and others don't?

Gurdjieff answered this for me, which I later confirmed in Jung's writing when he quoted the ancient alchemists that he studied thoroughly in his quest for his lost soul. Like the alchemists, Gurdjieff said that nature can only evolve man so far, and no further; and to become the person we are meant to be we have to take evolution into our own hands, which one could do with his teaching.

We have to complete what nature left unfinished because life is not enough to satisfy the longing in our soul for wholeness and singleness of self, which was why Katherine Mansfield sought Gurdjieff out and what the ancient alchemists attempted to satisfy with their abstruse teaching of conscious self-becoming that my hero C. G. Jung decoded and introduced to the modern world with his psychology of individuation; so it didn't matter how much Hemingway feasted on life with every pleasure that he sought as though it was his divine right, it would never have been enough to satisfy that hollow in his soul that he wrote about in "A Clean, Well-Lighted Place" when he was a still young man with his life ahead of him.

Hemingway had to get the most out of life to satisfy the longing in his soul to be the best writer that he could be, both in the ascent and descent of his every experience, and no man could have asked more of him; but it wasn't enough. That's what made him a tragic hero like the mythic Sisyphus condemned to the fate of his daily struggle, and in the end the unresolved *nada* of his successful life crushed his tormented soul and he blew himself to hell like his father before him; but even in his death there was certain grace, and for that I have to admire him.

12. The Hermetic Secret

Hemingway knew that there was something magical about writing that brought one closer to the secret that lies at the heart of life, but even the magic of writing could not bring him close enough to really see it.

In a 1952 letter to the critic Harvey Breit, Hemingway wrote: "...there is a mystery in all great writing and that mystery does not dis-sect out." And he said to his wife Mary, "Nobody really knows or understands and nobody has ever said the secret. The secret is that it is poetry written into prose and it is the hardest thing of all to do," but even the poets in all their genius have never really figured it out.

"I, you, he, she, we, /In the garden of mystic lovers, /these are not true distinctions," said the mystic poet Rumi; and in another poem he said, "These leaves, our bodily personalities, seem identical, /but the globe of soul-fruit /we make, /each is elaborately unique." This comes closest to the secret.

The Sufi poet Farid ud-Din Attar wrote an allegory of man's quest for the secret that lies at the heart of life, which he reveals to be the divine self of each and every soul, but he did not dis-sect the secret in his beautiful allegory *The Conference of the Birds*; and we're left with the mystical knowledge that soul is God.

I knew that from the poem I wrote in grade twelve. When God summoned Noman for a reckoning, I did not know what my poem meant; but when Noman was banished to the "fourth corner of the abyss" to look for God's "fish's scale," I came to realize that God had called me to find my lost soul; so the Sufi allegory, for all of its tantalizing mystic flavor, did not tell me anything new, and the secret continued to elude me. And then I read what John Keats wrote to his brother in his letter "The Vale of Soul Making," and I caught my first real glimpse of the secret that lies so deep in the heart of life that very few souls are privileged to see it.

"There may be intelligences or sparks of divinity in millions, but they are not Souls till they acquire identities, till each one is personally itself," wrote the poet who had touched the hem of God. "Intelligences are atoms of perception—they know and they see and they are pure; in short, they are God. How then are Souls to be made? How then are these sparks which are God to have identity given to them—so as even to possess a bliss to each one by individual existence? How but by the medium of a world like this?" (*Values*, J. G. Bennett, p.12)

My hero C. G. Jung realized this also when he wrote in the chronicle of his quest for his lost soul: "But one thing you must know: the one thing that I have learned is that one must live this life. This life is the way, the long sought-after way to the unfathomable, which we call divine. There is no other way, all other ways are false paths" (*The Red Book*, Reader's Edition, p. 128).

The secret is that we are all sparks of God seeking our own identity; but as Keats and Jung reveal, we have to go through the medium of life to realize the bliss of our own individuality. And herein lies the mystery, because nature can only evolve us so far and no further, and life after life after life we keep coming back to fulfill our destiny until we become so weary of life that we want out of the whole damn thing; and so we become seekers and look for the key to our prison door.

"There is a doctrine uttered in secret that man is a prisoner who has no right to open the door of his prison and run away," said Socrates in Plato's *Phaedo*; but Socrates found the key, which he revealed in his philosophy: *virtue*.

Socrates tells us that the only way out of the endless cycle of life and death, better known as the eternal wheel of karma and reincarnation, is by living a life of virtue; because only by transforming the consciousness of our lower self can we realize the consciousness of the spiritual self that we are. But why virtue?

Even Gurdjieff with all of his esoteric knowledge and genius for the secret teaching could not explain the inherently self-transcending power of virtue; and this is the secret that lies at the heart of life that can only be revealed to those who initiate themselves into the mystery but which all great writers and artists experience but cannot explain when they tap into the creative consciousness of life with their art.

The mystery of the secret is that it reveals itself whenever one taps into the creative consciousness of life, and so spiritually satisfying is the secret that one can never get enough of it; that's why writers *have* to write and painters *have* to paint and people *have* to do what they do when they have been called to their destiny.

Jung called the secret the *transcendent function*. But that only speaks to the inherently self-transcending power of the secret that resolves the consciousness of our *being* and *non-being*. Socrates called it "purification," and as one lives a life of virtue one activates the *transcendent function* of purification and individuates their lower and higher self into one harmonious spiritually self-realized self; just as Jesus taught with his teaching of salvation by being born again in Spirit.

"And what is purification but the separation of the soul from the body," said Socrates, "the habit of soul gathering and collecting herself, out of all the courses of the body; the dwelling in her own place alone, as in another life, so also in this, as far as she can; the release of the soul from the chains of the body?"

I "worked" on myself with Gurdjieff's teaching and Christ's sayings and activated the *transcendent function*; and the more I "worked" on myself, the more the secret revealed itself to me. This is how I came to realize that the more one lives the Way, the more the Way reveals itself to you; just as Hemingway became enlightened in the mystery of creative writing with every story that he wrote, because in the *doing* one *becomes*—which is the natural process of individuating the creative force of life. But life is not enough to individuate one's consciousness to the point of satisfying the longing in one's soul; and one can never realize wholeness and singleness of self through the natural process of experience alone—regardless how much life one feasts on, like my high school hero Hemingway.

Hemingway lived to live, and he never went one day without getting some enjoyment out of his life; but it was never enough to satisfy the longing in his soul that drove him to get the most out of life, despite the *transcendent function* of his creative genius that gave him more satisfaction than anything else that he did—even more than marlin fishing which challenged every fiber of his being. And like so many souls trapped by the *enantiodromiac* dilemma of their life, my high school hero ended his life badly; but not my other hero C. G. Jung.

At the age of forty Jung was no longer pulled by life to satisfy the longing in his soul to be the person he was meant to be, because life could no longer satisfy his longing through the natural process of individuation which could take him no further. He wrote in *The Red Book*: "Then my desire for the increase of these trappings ('honor, power, wealth, knowledge, and every human happiness') ceased, the desire ebbed from me and horror came over me." And then he heard "the spirit of the depths," which he did not understand. Yet "the spirit of the depths" drove him with unbearable inner longing, and in despair he cried out: "My soul, where are you? Do you hear me? I speak, I call you—are you there? I have returned. I am here again..." And Jung sank into the depths of his unconscious to begin the quest for his lost soul, thereby taking the natural individuation process of his life into his own hands and actively participating in his own becoming to complete what nature could not finish— the exact opposite of what my literary mentor did with his life.

With incredible zest for life, Hemingway grabbed all the life he could to satisfy the longing in his soul to be the person he was meant to be, even to the point of falling desperately and foolishly in love with an aristocratic young beauty who became the model for Renata in his novel *Across the River and Into the Trees*, the nineteen year old Venetian Adriana Ivancich; but his young muse could not satisfy his inner longing, because the natural process of individuation cannot satisfy one's longing for wholeness and singleness of self, and despite all the women in his selfish and needy life Hemingway was always left wanting. As Jung came to realize in the fortieth year of his accomplished life, life simply wasn't enough; and rather than continue his life as it was, getting more and more of the same like Hemingway tried to do every time he fell in love with another woman, Jung had a *metanoiac* change of heart and "put his hand to the plow" and went in search of his lost soul.

In my heart I knew that it wasn't how much life I lived that would satisfy my longing for my true self, it was the kind of life that I lived; that's why I *had* to become a seeker first and writer second. And with Gurdjieff's teaching of "work on oneself" I initiated myself into the mysteries of life until one day the hermetic secret at the heart of life revealed itself to me, and I was shocked by the magnificence of its simplicity as I grew into the person that I was meant to be; and when I'm called upon to reveal this hermetic secret, I will gladly do so—quite possibly in my last chapter, after I've resolved the mystery of why I was called back to Hemingway.

13. Writing Through Crazy

"The mind is its own place, and in itself can make a hell of heaven, a heaven of hell," said John Milton in *Paradise Lost*; and for years, ever since I awakened the "serpent fire" that night in Annecy, France my life was a private hell; and the only way out was to write my way through the crazy world of my own making.

One day while on my way to give an estimate for a painting job I saw a young man I knew standing on the street corner in front of the only restaurant in town talking to himself. His lips weren't moving, but I knew he was talking to himself; and it was raining. I wanted to stop and have a good sound talk with him; but I had an appointment with a potential customer.

Thirty or forty minutes later, on my way home from my appointment, I saw Brent still standing on the street corner still talking to himself. I pulled alongside and opened my passenger door and said, "Get in, Brent; I want to talk with you."

He looked at me with a quizzical stare, water dripping off his nose but totally oblivious to the rain, and I repeated: "Get in the car, Brent!"

He got in and shut the door. I pulled out and drove down the street and on up through town to the Trans-Canada Highway; and not beating around the bush, I turned to him and said: "I know what you're doing. I know you're talking to yourself, Brent; and you have to stop it before it destroys your life."

Startled, he didn't know what to say; but I read his mind: *How could he know that I was talking to myself? He can't know.* But I did, and I felt sorry for him. He had gone too deep into his own mind and needed help.

Brent was the oldest of three children of a well-to-do family in town, and he was married with young children of his own; but he was still into drugs from his college days and had trouble holding down a job. His wife had a steady job and supported the family. I often saw him in one of the local bars with a group of friends, but even with his friends I would see him withdraw into the secret world of his own mind and have his private conversations; but no one knew but me.

I had seen this behavior before in the city malls whenever Penny and I drove up for our weekend shopping; people sitting alone talking to themselves, at first silently but eventually audibly; but they couldn't help themselves and no longer cared. One man well-known throughout the city could be seen walking down the street having a grand old time talking away to himself; but he wasn't talking to himself, he was talking to people in his own mind whom he thought were real.

We had a young native man who lived on the reservation outside our town but who came into town once or twice a week, and he babbled away to himself all the time. I even wrote a short story called "Babbles" just to see how it would turn out; and I got the surprise of my life, because this story revealed to me for the first time in my writing life the real power of the creative unconscious when the story magically gave birth to its own reality by taking my fictional Babbles to a place I could not have imagined, like the story gave birth to its own solution.

This story gave me the confidence to trust the creative process, because it had a mind of its own that was far superior to mine; and though inspired by a real person, my story had a satisfying fictional ending. Brent was real too, and I had no idea how his life was going to end; but I feared for him.

"I know what you're doing, Brent. I've been there, and living in your own mind is a very dangerous place to be. The people you're talking to in your mind aren't real. You may think they're real, but they're not. They're only psychic projections, and all you're doing is feeding them and keeping them alive. You need help, Brent. You can't stop this on your own. You have to get professional help."

Startled, Brent stared at me completely nonplussed. I continued: "You've fooled a lot of people, Brent; but you can't go on like this. It's going to ruin your life. It almost ruined mine. I don't mean to scare you, but the more you continue to live in your own mind the harder it's going to be to stop." Two weeks later they found his body in a hotel room; he had overdosed.

When I was living in Annecy, France I got sucked into a very dangerous habit that began because of a foolish experiment with the Ouija board that my friend was given by another friend who was afraid to have it in her house. My friend wanted to experiment, and we did make contact with something the first time we tried; but this experiment opened me up to mischievous psychic influences, and before I knew it I was doing what I thought was automatic writing, and I would spend hours in my little apartment letting these "psychic entities" come through on paper.

My hand became sore from all the writing, and soon I began to let these "entities" speak to me in my mind; and the more I indulged in this ego-projecting habit, the more I got pulled into a fantasy world of my own making. That's how it all started. Back in Canada I couldn't stop the habit, and I masked my escape into the fantasy world of my own mind by carrying a notebook with me everywhere I went; I would sit in restaurants or wherever and play out my fantasies on paper. No one was the wiser, and I did this for years, even after I began "working" on myself with Gurdjieff's teaching; and, believe me, I had a lot to "work" on.

My fantasy world was no different than a creative writer's world when he's working on a novel, but with one critical difference: I was the wizard who conjured up my own reality to suit my own egoic needs, whereas a novel creates its own reality apart from the writer's control but with the writer's willful consent; and unless I built up the strength to properly channel the irrepressible energies of the "serpent fire" that I had awakened in Annecy, I feared I might get sucked so deep into my fantasy world that I would never find my way out again.

81

That was my dilemma that took me the better part of ten years to resolve, which I could not have done without Gurdjieff's teaching. I ordered every book that I could get on Gurdjieff the man and his teaching from *Samuel Weiser, Inc.* in New York City, starting with Gurdjieff's own books first (*The Herald of Coming Good, Meetings with Remarkable Men, All and Everything, Life Is Only Real Then, When 'I Am'* and *Views from the Real World*), and I dove into them like my life depended upon it, which it did; and book by book, month by month, and inspiration by inspiration provided by Gurdjieff's remarkable students like Doctor Maurice Nicoll, who studied under Carl Jung before going to the *Institute for the Harmonious Development of Man* who wrote the *Psychological Commentaries on the Teachings of Gurdjieff and Ouspensky*, Thomas and Olga de Harmann's memoir *Our Life with Mr. Gurdjieff*, the journals of C. S. Nott, Margaret Anderson's memoir *The Unknowable Gurdjieff*, Kathryn Hulme's *Undiscovered Country, In Search of Gurdjieff*, all of J. G. Bennett's books on Gurdjieff, Fritz Peters' memoir *Gurdjieff Remembered*, all of Ouspensky's books, *On Love*, by the brilliant editor A. R. Orage who introduced me to Katherine Mansfield's short stories, and dozens of other students of Gurdjieff's teaching who all gave me the feeling that I was part of this remarkable inner circle of dedicated seekers; and I slowly began to build the moral fortitude to channel my erratic energies into my outer life instead of having them consumed by my insatiable egoic desires in a fantasy world of my own making.

But I didn't "work" on myself in a vacuum. I started my own painting business and did everything possible to get all the work that I could hustle because I needed all the contact with the real world that I could get to keep from being sucked into the fantasy world of my own mind; and I kept a notebook in my shirt pocket to channel my creative juices which became notes for possible future stories, until one day I was informed by a friend that my customers were afraid to talk to me because they thought I was taking notes on what we talked about and I had to stop the habit of pulling my notebook out while working in my customer's home and went out to my van instead whenever the urge possessed me, something but not quite like Joyce used to do when he dashed off to the washroom to jot down furtive notes on the people he was drinking with in the Dublin pubs that he later worked into *Dubliners* and his great novel *Ulysses*; that's how I wrote myself through the crazy world of my own mind as I "worked" on myself with Gurdjieff's teaching.

And now like my literary mentor who played out his fantasies in the stories that he wrote, like his unrequited love for the nurse Agnes von Kurowsky, his first real love who broke his young heart but whose love he idealized through Catherine Barkley in his wartime novel *A Farewell to Arms*, and his obsessive infatuation with the beautiful young Venetian Adriana Ivancich whom he called Renata in *Across the River and Into the Trees*, and his androgynous sexual impulses that he played out in *The Garden of Eden*, and his perennial struggle with his *shadow* self in *The Old Man and the Sea,* I write fiction; because a writer has to make it up in order to be able to tell the truth; and I have many stories yet to be written.

14. The Call of Soul

My high school hero Ernest Hemingway was called to writing, as C. G. Jung was called to pioneer the fledgling discipline of psychotherapy and I was called to become a seeker first and writer second; but just what does it mean to be called?

James Hillman attributes the call to the "acorn theory," saying that we are all encoded with what we are meant to be; but how did we become encoded?

Biology certainly determines our physical makeup, and even though hard science would like us to believe that our genes make us what we are (as they continue to look for the "gay" gene, the "poetry" gene, and the "everything" gene), I've come to believe that there's much more to our life than our physical body; which is why I had to become a seeker first despite myself—*because I had to know why.*

In my early twenties I did extensive reading on reincarnation, my favorite books being on Edgar Cayce, who was known as "the sleeping prophet" because he would go into a trance and read a person's past lives, and he did psychic readings for one's health as well, for which he developed such a reputation that people from all over the world consulted him for their health; and then I read a book by Jess Stearn called *The Search for the Soul: Psychic Lives of Taylor Caldwell,* which was the story of the historical novelist's past lives that were recorded from her past-life regressions; and no sooner did I finish reading this book and knew that one day I would write a book on my own past lives, and that day came when Penny and I relocated to Georgian Bay when by "chance" I met a past-life regressionist.

I had seven past-life regressions and wrote my book, and the title *Cathedral of My Past Lives* was given to me by a friend who saw the cover of my book in one of her psychic visions; but I put it aside where it's still waiting for the editorial revision that all manuscripts need upon first completion. Nonetheless, because of my seven past-life regressions I managed to resolve the mystery of why we're called to our destiny; and as difficult as it may be to believe, I'm bound by the literary credo that I adopted from my high school hero to tell it the way it happened to me.

As I said, in my teens I had at least three past-life recollection dreams; but they did not explain the feelings I had about my family. Deep inside I knew that my relationship with my family was past-life related, and my first regression resolved the mystery of why I felt the way I did about my parents and siblings; but that's all in my novel *Cathedral of My Past Lives*, and I need not expound upon it here.

David Mitchel wrote an amazing novel called *Cloud Atlas*, which is a very complex story about reincarnation that was adapted into a movie starring the ubiquitous Tom Hanks; but in an interview the author revealed that he did not believe in reincarnation, and his novel would have had to be a phenomenal feat of creative writing which I personally believe implies much more than the author will ever know because the creative unconscious has a mind of its own. But my novel *Cathedral of My Past Lives* was drawn primarily from my seven past-life regressions, and whether one sees it as an elaborate exercise of my own fertile imagination doesn't really matter to the evolution of literary fiction; but like my high school hero who won the hearts and minds of countless readers with stories drawn from his own richly conflicted life experiences, *Cathedral of My Past Lives* was also drawn from the incredible experience of my past-life regressions, and I did everything creatively possible to make the impalpable palpable to satisfies the conscience of my literary credo. What then did I experience that resolves the inscrutable mystery of why we are all called to our destiny?

It happened with my sixth past-life regression. I went back, back, and back through time and before time and before life began to where we all come from in the Eternal Body of God,

85

which in the poetic language of the spiritual path that I embraced after I outgrew Gurdjieff's teaching and which prepared me for my own path of creative writing is called the "Ocean of Love and Mercy," and I experienced myself as I was before I was sent into this world to acquire my own identity.

I was an atom of God in the Body of God, but I did not have self-identity; I was an un-self-realized soul seed, and after I experienced what it was like to be an atom of God without a reflective self-consciousness, I was sent down into Planet Earth to evolve through life until I realized my own identity.

It took a while to figure out how I could experience myself as an atom of God if I did not have a reflective self-consciousness; but as I wrote my novel it finally came to me that I was my self-realized self when I was regressed to myself as an un-self-realized atom of God, and I had the dual consciousness of the alpha and omega of my soul self that I had evolved into, which was precisely the information that Carl Jung had come to talk to me about in my dream, because he could not fathom the alpha and omega of man's central archetype which he called the Self.

After I experienced the ineffable bliss of being an un-self-realized atom of God in the great Ocean of Love and Mercy, I was sent into the Earth world to experience evolution up the ladder of life all the way up to my lifetime as a higher primate where I experienced the birth of the individuating consciousness of my reflective self. I actually experienced the birth of my own "I" which separated me from my group consciousness and filled me with such longing to be that I cannot explain the profound depths of the unbearable agony to be more me; and thus began my karmic destiny from life to life until I realized wholeness and singleness of self.

I was the alpha male of a small group of higher primates; and as the alpha male I was the dominant leader who controlled my group with brute force and power grunts. I kept them all in check by constantly grunting; and if they didn't obey I beat them savagely and cowered them into submission. But as obvious as this alpha behavior is to people who study the social behavior of animal groups today, what they don't realize is the exchange of energy that goes on with this behavior that fuels the natural process of individuating the consciousness of life and which in our modern world can be seen in the power that people assert over others, like the husband who has to have his way with his wife and children or there will be hell to pay; or—and, please forgive me for going there—the kind of controlling behavior that my high school hero displayed with every one of his four wives, because he fed off their energies to fuel the creative genius of his writing until he exhausted them and had to find a new "muse," all but Martha Gellhorn, that is; because she refused to be used that way by the selfish writer and left him to pursue her own career and grow in her own identity. That's why she said, "I am not an appendage to someone else's life," implying the great writer who could not keep her in her place at their home *La Finca Vigia* with him when she wanted to be her own person too.

Gurdjieff had an insight into this mysterious exchange of energies between people, and he evolved his insight into a teaching that he called "the way of the sly man." But very few of his students understood "the way of the sly man," because one has to have "eyes" to see how people appropriate another person's will-to-be so they can grow in their own identity—like Hemingway's attitude towards people, always competing for that subtle life force that he needed to grow into the great writer that he wanted to be. It was primordial, and it puzzled those who loved him; but in the end it destroyed his life because there is a great karmic price to pay when one uses people this way. And that's why I parted ways with Hemingway.

Jesus taught "the way of the sly man" also, but Jesus was much more discerning of how to "catch" the subtle life force that we need to grow into the wholeness and singleness of self that we are meant to be, which I expound upon in my book *Why Bother? The Riddle of the Good Samaritan*. The point is that I experienced the birth of my reflective self in my regression, and this gave me the final piece to the puzzle of why we are; and after I wrote *Cathedral of My Past Lives* I ceased to be burdened by the riddle of life.

So, why are we called then? Jesus said to Glenda Green in her book *Love without End, Jesus Speaks*—the phenomenal story of how Jesus came to Glenda Green so she could paint his portrait, which she called "The Lamb and the Lion"—that *"there is only the self and God,"* and after I wrote *Cathedral of My Past Lives* I understood what Jesus meant, because God grows in the consciousness of God through the evolution of its atoms through life; and with the birth of every new "I" of God in man we are called to our spiritual destiny of realizing our own identity.

Or so this story goes...

15. Hemingway's Literary Ideal

"The most essential gift for a good writer is a built-in, shockproof, shit detector. This is a writer's radar and all great writers have it," Hemingway told George Plimpton in an interview for *The Paris Review* in the spring of 1958.

My mentor was obsessed with authenticity, which is why he built his literary credo upon his "one true sentence" principle; and he went out of his way to be as true to his experience of life as he could be. This is how he became so knowledgeable in everything that he took an interest in, like fishing, hunting, boxing, and especially bullfighting which obsessed him with its tragic drama of life and death.

"Good writing is true writing. If a man is making a story up it will be true in proportion to the amount of knowledge of life that he has and how conscientious he is; so that when he makes something up it is as it would truly be," he wrote in *Esquire* magazine, October 1935; but what did my mentor mean for something made up to be "as it would truly be"? Was he looking for some kind of Platonic ideal?

This is the heart of Hemingway's literary ideal, and it speaks to the mystical nature of writing; because for a story to be "as it would truly be" a writer has to trust his own creative judgment, which is not an easy thing to do. But like all writers, Hemingway knew that the more he wrote the more he would know if he got it right or not; but to hedge his bets, Hemingway leaned on Lady Luck to get it right after doing everything that he could do to make his story "as it would truly be."

Scholars have studied Hemingway's style from the day he broke convention and became a literary force unto himself, and after all the reading that I have done on his life (in and out of every story that he wrote), I've come to see that my literary mentor did with every story he wrote what Michelangelo did with every piece of marble that he sculpted: he chipped away at it until he was left with nothing but the perfect image that he saw with his mind's eye locked inside the piece of marble.

Hemingway's style has been called terse, taut, lean, simple, unadorned, spare, elegant, "cablese" (which refers to the pared down sentences that he used when he dispatched news stories by cable from Europe to North America), and many other words in an effort to pin down his style; but all he was trying to do was get his readers to see and feel the essential truth of the experience that he was writing about; which meant the least obfuscation in his style that he could affect. Like the great artist who chipped away all the extraneous pieces of his solid slab of marble to get to the perfect image of his David or Madonna and Child, so too did Hemingway pare down his stories until he was left with the perfect ideal of his story experience.

Hemingway pared down his stories so effectively that he caught a glimpse of the secret that lies buried at the heart of life; which was why he said to his fourth wife Mary, "Nobody really knows or understands and nobody has ever said the secret. The secret is that it is poetry written into prose and it is the hardest of all things to do..." And this is the mystical nature of Hemingway's writing that has captured the hearts and minds of generations of readers; but again, what is this secret that he and so many writers and artists touch upon? Or, as Hemingway implied, what was the carcass of that leopard doing near the summit of the House of God?

In his book *C. G. Jung and Herman Hesse, A Record of Two Friendships*, Miguel Serrano had a conversation with Jung late in Jung's life, shortly before Jung passed over to the other side; and Jung tried to explain the central message of his psychology, which he defined as the mystical union of the individuation process; but he had trouble putting it to words, and with a far-away look, "as though in a trance," he said to Miguel Serrano:

"Nobody understands what I mean. Only a poet could begin to understand...the path is very difficult."

One of the cruelest lessons that was forced upon me by life, both personal and literary, is that it is highly commendable for one to seek this secret that lies hidden in the heart of life but not commendable to find it. One can read all the books and go on a quest throughout the world like so many seekers do and write about it like Paulo Coelho did with his bestselling allegory *The Alchemist* that touched the archetypal seeker in all of us, or push oneself with such *daemonic* passion in one's art until one collapses with exhaustion time and again, which is all very laudable and much respected; but one must never find this secret hidden in the heart of life, because should one find the secret one will no longer be treated the same again. One becomes suspect, and everything one says and does is instinctively resisted, because it threatens the very core of who and what people are; which was why so many people that Hemingway wrote about felt betrayed, as did the people of my hometown who saw themselves in the dark *shadow* personality of my community in the characters of my provocative novel *What Would I Say Today if I Were to Die Tomorrow?* and turned on me like a dog rudely awakened from a deep sleep.

In November 1915 Carl Jung wrote a letter to Hans Schmid that explains this peculiar trait in man to resist knowing the truth about himself. "...after long reflection, the problem of *resistance to understanding* has clarified itself to me," he wrote; and it was clarified by a vision that Brigitta of Sweden (1303-1373) had when she saw the devil who spoke to God. Jung learned from the mystic's vision that *understanding is a devourer that swallows you up.* "The core of the individual is a mystery of life, which is snuffed out when it is 'grasped,'" wrote Jung; and to understand a person's private self leaves one feeling like he has been "murdered," which is why people have such a resistance to be understood for who and what they truly are. They don't want to be seen. They don't want to be found out. They don't want to be understood. They want to hold onto their personal mystery.

This is why my hometown turned on me; I had revealed the dark *shadow* personality of my community in my novel and "murdered" it with the light of understanding.

But it took a long time for me to see that people prefer the certainty of not knowing to the reality of who and what they truly are; that's what has made writers and artist so feared and revered throughout history—because they *have* to stand upon the certainty of their truth. Why else would writers and artists be the first to be thrown into prison when governments are overthrown by dictators? Writers and artists are Keepers of the Flame and are obligated to tell the truth. That's what made Hemingway so goddamn frustrating to everyone who knew him; because he stood on the certainty of his truth of life, which was vast given the range of his personal experience. This is why writers write fiction. With the creative genius of their imagination they magnify life so that it can be seen for what it truly is and fulfill what Jung believed to be the sole purpose of human existence, which is to "kindle a candle in the darkness of mere being." This is why Shelly said in his iconic essay *A Defense of Poetry,* "Poets are the unacknowledged legislators of the world."

When Bill Moyers asked Adrienne Rich to define poetry, she replied: *"Poetry is an act of the imagination that transforms reality into a deeper perception of what is."* This holds true for prose as well, and *"what is"* is the secret that lies at the heart of life that Hemingway sought with every story that he wrote.

"What is" was Hemingway's literary ideal; but what did Adrienne Rich mean by this poetic phrase that seems to be the closest that writers and artists can get to the essential truth of all of life's experiences?

I worked in a bush camp one summer in my late teens cutting spruce and pine trees with a chain saw which I piled into eight foot length cord piles. I don't recall what I got paid, but I think it was eight dollars per cord; so the more trees I cut and piled, the more money I made. I was given my own strip of trees to cut, and when that was all cut the foreman would move me to a new strip. One day I came across a huge pine in a little gully, but I couldn't cord my wood there because it would be too hard to log out; so I had to make my pile on the flat ground above the gully.

I cut the pine to fall on the incline of the little hill, but the biggest and heaviest pieces of eight foot lengths would be at the bottom of the gully; and getting those pieces to the top of the incline brought to mind the great Sisyphean struggle.

After I cut all the limbs off the tree with my heavy Pioneer 620, I measured out the first eight foot length of the tree closest to the trunk, and it was so big that I did not know if I could up-end it to the top of the hill; but I would leave that till last. I cut the whole tree into six or seven eight-foot lengths and stopped to take a long drink of water; and then I began to up-end the logs up the incline to my new pile.

The first two or three logs were not that hard to up-end up to my pile, but as I descended the little hill to get the next piece I began to feel what Sisyphus must have felt as he descended to meet his fate again; but unlike Sisyphus whose rock was always the same size and weight, each log that I had to up-end to the top of the hill was bigger and heavier than the last; and each log challenged me.

But I was determined to pile the whole tree, and I summoned all the strength I could to up-end every log up the little hill and stack on my new pile; but the second last piece almost killed me. I was drenched in sweat and stopped to drink my still ice-cold water from my Javex bottle that I refilled every night and put into the freezer for the next day's work, and then I descended for the last piece.

I had to up-end it nine or ten times to my pile, but the first time I up-ended it I nearly died; and to this day I don't know how I did it, but I managed to stack that last piece of wood on my pile and then I stopped work for the day.

Albert Camus used Sisyphus's fate as a metaphor for man's daily struggles with life, and he imagined Sisyphus happy in his fate because for Camus the struggle itself was enough to fill a man's heart. As I up-ended each log up my little hill and stacked on my pile I definitely felt a sense of accomplishment that filled my heart with the joy of satisfaction, and when I descended for the next log I felt the dread of having to do it all over again, but with more effort each time because my logs got heavier; but I was bound and determined not to let the tree beat me.

With Camus' Sisyphus on my mind, the big pine tree became my metaphor for life; and I would up-end each eight-foot length up the hill and stack it on my pile because I was not going to let life get the best of me. So each log that I up-ended to the top of the hill became a daily struggle, and I struggled and struggled until I accomplished my task and piled the whole tree; and my heart was filled with joy.

Drenched in sweat, I sat and leaned my back on a tree and drank my still ice cold water and basked in my accomplishment as I thought of my buddy Sisyphus; but the more I thought of his absurd fate, the more I had to disagree with the philosopher who imagined Sisyphus happy in his struggle for all eternity.

"That's bullshit," I said to myself. "How can he be happy doing that for eternity? There has to be some meaning to our daily struggle. It can't all be for nothing. That's not fair. There has to be a meaning..."

That summer as a young man I experienced the *"what is"* of the Sisyphean struggle, both the joy of satisfaction and the dread of endless effort, but unlike the philosopher writer that I had grown to love I came to a different conclusion.

I experienced the joy of satisfaction that came when I accomplished my task, and this joy not only filled my heart but fed my soul because in my joy I felt more complete and more myself; and many years later, long after I had lived Gurdjieff's teaching and found my true self, when I read what Jung had to say about the way in his *Red Book* I was brought back to my Sisyphean struggle with my tree and I knew with absolute gnostic certainty that he was right to say that "this life is the way, the long sought-after way to the unfathomable, which we call divine."

Life is a struggle. This is an irrefutable existential fact. But what I experienced that summer with my literal and metaphorical tree gave me an insight into our daily struggles that no one could take away from me. Our struggles feed our soul so we can grow into the person we are meant to be, which is what Jesus meant when he said to Philemon in Jung's *Red Book* that he had brought man "the beauty of suffering," because through the suffering of our daily struggles we nourish our primal need for self-identity; and life is not meaningless and absurd.

"All the growth is in the hassle," said a teacher of the Way, and that summer at Camp 81 in the forests of Northwestern Ontario, I experienced the *"what is"* of the Sisyphean struggle and learned the secret of my mentor's literary ideal, because in the *"what is"* of every human experience can be found the *enantiodromiac* truth of life that feeds our soul with purpose and meaning; but, as Katherine Mansfield came to see, the *"what is"* of literature is not enough to satisfy our need to be the person we are meant to be, and this was Hemingway's personal quandary.

Like the mythical hero of ancient Greece, the "cleverest of men" who cheated the gods and condemned himself to Hades, the cleverest of writers also condemned himself to his own Sisyphean struggle, and in the end the unbearable burden of his own insufferable karmic fate wore his mind and body down and beat him; but like his hero Santiago in *The Old Man and the Sea* it could not destroy his indomitable spirit, and this is the magnetic appeal of Hemingway's literary ideal.

16. An *Enantiodromiac* Force

I would never have gone back to Hemingway had I not been strongly nudged by that inner force that has guided my life ever since I can remember to watch the movie *Hemingway and Gellhorn* while Penny and our guests ate dinner at the kitchen table, because something about the way Hemingway and his third wife Marty, as she was called, were portrayed—which spoke to the talent of the actors that captured the essence of their characters—revealed the *"what is"* of their relationship and resolved the mystery of Hemingway's paradoxical personality

Like all of his relationships with his wives since Hadley, Hemingway had an affair with them first while he was still married, and all but one of his wives divorced him; Martha Gellhorn was the only one who left Hemingway and he filed for divorce on grounds of desertion because she was always off on journalism assignments, and Hemingway never forgave her for this humiliating blow to his macho image.

But Martha Gellhorn had enough of the great Hemingway and his bloated ego and pathological lying and vicious verbal cruelties and neurotic need to mold her into the kind of wife that only served his needs like he had molded his first two wives Hadley and Pauline, and as he went on to do with his fourth wife Mary with whom he had an affair while still married to Martha; and to satisfy her own compulsive inner need to be the person that she was meant to be, Martha had to leave him because the selfish writer had become a dangerous threat to her identity. "I am not an appendage to someone else's life," she asserted many years later.

Unlike Hadley who devoted her married life and precious energy to nursing Hemingway's writing career, and Pauline, once secure in her conviction that she had stolen Hemingway from Hadley, who wrote to tell him "I am going to look out for you and after you and I won't have anything else to do but try to please you," Martha, who in turn stole Hemingway from Pauline, wanted to pursue her own writing career to satisfy her inherent need to be the person she felt compelled to be; but her ambition proved to be the source of all their contention, and sooner or later their marriage was bound to blow up in their face, exactly as the movie *Hemingway and Gellhorn* revealed. But why did I have this compulsion to watch the story of Hemingway's tempestuous relationship with his ambitious third wife who went on to become an iconic role model for women? What was my inner guidance trying to tell me?

Because I was a seeker first who had the good fortune to find my true self, I came to see that of all our needs in life—air, water, food, sex, shelter, and our need to be loved—our greatest need is to become the person we are meant to be; so everything that we do in life goes to nourishing our inherent need for self-identity, and everyone that touched Hemingway's life served this need.

"Mary didn't seem to realize," said Hotchner, the author of *Papa Hemingway*, to Denis Brian for his book *The True Gen, An Intimate Portrait of Hemingway by Those Who Knew Him*, "that a writer is an undisciplined animal who will write about anything that touches his life," and absolutely nothing was sacred to Hemingway—except perhaps his first wife Hadley, whom he could never bring himself to forgive for losing a valise full of all his early writing but whose love for her he so revered that shortly before taking his own life he confessed in *A Moveable Feast* that he wished he had died rather than love anyone but her.

Hemingway was an *enantiodromiac* force that exploded upon the scene of life with his literary career, but I had no idea what kind of force this was until I watched the movie of his contentious relationship with Martha Gellhorn; this is why shortly after watching the movie I was nudged to look up the word *enantiodromia* that I had come across in Jung's book *Modern Man in Search of a Soul* and explore its profound psychological meaning. And the more research I did on this Heraclitean principle, the more I discerned what Jung meant by the process of individuation central to his psychology, and the more I understood my high school hero; but what exactly did Jung mean by this mysterious principle of *enantiodromia*?

In Heraclitus' philosophy, *enantiodromia* is used to designate the play of opposites in the events of life; the view that everything that exists eventually turns into its opposite—light into dark, heat into cold, life into death, good into evil, true into false, yes into no and no into yes, and so on; a never-ending play of what the Taoists call the Yin and Yang of life, a drama of endless becoming.

"I use the term *enantiodromia* for the emergence of the unconscious opposite in the course of time," wrote Jung; and by this he meant that this fundamental principle of life occurs in man when an extreme one-sided tendency dominates our conscious personality and in time an equally powerful counter-position is built up in our unconscious, which first inhibits our conscious ego and subsequently breaks through our conscious control and takes over our personality, as Hemingway amply demonstrated throughout his life with his paradoxical behavior, especially in his later years when his *shadow* could be "switched" on with the least provocation.

In *Paris without End, The True Story of Hemingway's First Wife*, Gioia Diliberto wrote that Hadley's account of her marriage contradicts the view of her husband typically expressed by his biographers that he was domineering, neglectful, and often cruel. Hadley, who did not like to talk about her husband's moody, dark side, accented his good side: "Ernest was loving, affectionate, and sweet," and he was deeply interested in her life and her happiness; but his third wife Martha Gellhorn told Denis Brian for his book *The True Gen* that he was "one of the cruelest men I ever knew," and to stress her point she added, "and believe me I've known an awful lot of them," And Jack Hemingway, Earnest and Hadley's son, told Denis Brian, "That's the way we Hemingways are. We're nice guys one day and sons-of-bitches the next," alluding to the root cause of the famous "Hemingway curse."

This paradoxical trait made the evolving young writer an *enantiodromiac* force that has puzzled the world; but as I watched the movie *Hemingway and Gellhorn* the mystery of the *enantiodromiac* play of opposites that was played out large on the movie screen by Clive Owen and Nicole Kidman resolved itself before my eyes, and I exclaimed, *"That's it! He had to have that to become a great writer! Hemingway had to be a prick to become the great writer that he became!"*

In a sudden flash of insight, I saw that whenever Hemingway's blind, selfish, and viciously cruel *shadow* sprang free from the depths of his unconscious and took over his personality all hell would break loose; and the sparks that flew fueled the flame of his creative genius. That's why he had to be a prick to become the great writer that he became; and this was a pattern that he repeated with all of his wives, not just with the fiercely independent Martha Gellhorn who insisted on paying her own way in her tempestuous marriage with the great Ernest Hemingway.

"Each trip down his emotional roller coaster took him deeper into his private demons," wrote the biographer Michael Reynolds in *Hemingway the Final Years*. "Each time down, it was more difficult to climb back up. But each time he recovered, his writing exploded." But each time down, he lost ground to his *shadow*; and when it came out it wanted to stay out. That's why he had to have shock treatment.

Hemingway was larger than life. War veteran, big game hunter, deep-sea fisherman, bullfighting aficionado, boxer, four-time husband and father of three, incorrigible womanizer, war correspondent, writer for *Esquire* and other prestigious magazines, master short story writer, novelist and winner of the Nobel Prize for Literature, he strutted through life like a literary titan; but as brilliant and complex as he was, his winning charismatic personality had a very dark and menacing *shadow* side, and when it came out it wrought havoc in his life. That's what made my high school hero and literary mentor an *enantiodromiac* force that has grabbed the imagination of generations of readers, and will continue to do so; because reading Hemingway is an experience that awakens one to their true nature. As he said in the December, 1934 issue of *Esquire*, "All good books are alike in that they are truer than if they had really happened and after you are finished reading one you will feel that all happened to you." That's why I was called back to Hemingway.

17. The Lion that Swallowed Hemingway

The damn thing about the *shadow* side of our personality is that it has a mind of its own and we can't see it. Like Jung said, "How can you find a lion that has swallowed you?" But we can sense its presence, like I began to do in grade ten when I started to experience those strange impulses to be false.

Curiously enough however, the *shadow* side of our personality is not invisible to others; and despite how much our *shadow* self tries to hide itself in our conscious ego-personality, there will always be someone who sees it for what it's not; and what it's not is our true, authentic self. This is why Martha Gellhorn called her great writer husband an "apocryphiar," because the more she got to know him, the more intimate she became with the false *shadow* side of his personality.

In his novel *Islands in the Stream*, Hemingway says something about Thomas Hudson's deck hand that points to Hemingway's awareness of the *shadow*: "Well, I guess that is enough of that, Thomas Hudson thought. I better leave it as it lays and go back to the stern and watch my other problem child come aboard. I can never feel about Peters the way the rest of them all feel. I hope I know as well as they do what his defects are. But he has something. *He is like the false carried so far that it is made true.* It is certain that he is not up to handling what we have. But maybe he is up to much better things" (*Islands in the Stream*, p. 376, italics mine).

Like everyone else—actually, he was much more aware than everyone else, because he was a very clever writer who had trained himself to observe every facet of human nature—Hemingway could spot the false side of a person's personality, as his alter ego Thomas Hudson spotted his deck hand's false self, which was why he had such a passion for the real and great detestation for the false, especially when it came to writing. "A writer who omits things because he does not know them only makes hollow places in his writing," he wrote in *Death in the Afternoon*, which was why he called Katherine Mansfield's stories near-beer. They lacked the requisite amount of authenticity to give them the flavor of real beer, and felt hollow. But, ironically, Hemingway was so blind to his own hollow self that in the end he lost control of the *shadow* side of his personality and it destroyed his life.

This was the tragic flaw of the great writer's character, a flaw that we all have because we all have a *shadow* side; but because Hemingway had such an expansive personality immensely rich in life experience, his *shadow* was so big and ravenous in its hunger to *be* that it easily dominated his ego-personality, especially when drinking because alcohol has a way of flipping the "switch" that sets the *shadow* free from the deep recesses of our psyche, and Hemingway loved to drink.

But for all of his heavy drinking, Hemingway had disciplined himself to not let it destroy his talent like it destroyed his friend's precious gift; and as unflattering as he knew it was going to be, he told it as it was with the friend who helped launch his career at *Scribners* in his painfully written and painful to read chapter "Scott Fitzgerald" in his memoir *A Moveable Feast*: "His talent was as natural as the pattern that was made by the dust on a butterfly's wings. At one time he understood it no more than the butterfly did and he did not know when it was brushed or marred. Later he became conscious of his damaged wings and of their construction and he learned to think and could not fly anymore because the love of flight was gone and he could only remember when it had been effortless" (*A Moveable Feast*, p. 145); and then he goes on with a vicious anecdote that revealed how his friend was affected by alcohol which brushed and marred the writer's wings.

That's why my high school hero became my literary mentor, despite the fact that the more I got to know about the man the more I grew to hate him, until I saw the movie *Hemingway and Gellhorn* that is; because Clive Owen's and

Nicole Kidman's brilliant portrayal of the great writer and his recalcitrant wife opened up a window onto Hemingway's soul that introduced me to the *enantiodromiac* principle of life that fuels the natural process of individuation that drives our destiny to become the person we are meant to be, and herein lies the central mystery of Hemingway's perplexing paradoxical personality.

How could a writer so obsessive about truth in his writing be so obversely different in his non-writing personality? How could he be so true in his craft and be a self-aggrandizing apocryphiar who cheated on his wives in his everyday life? Could he not see the painfully obvious distinctive shades of his own personality? And did he have to write to absolve his conscience for not being true?

That's what frustrated the hell out of his four wives and perplexed and hurt his family, alienated his friends, and drove every scholar that studied his life and work to scratch their head in vain; and it bedeviled me all of my life until I saw the movie that gave me an insight that helped resolve the beguiling riddle of his bifurcated personality. But in all honesty, I would never have solved the mystery of Hemingway's personality had I not resolved the issue of my own *shadow*.

In his essay "On the Psychology of the Unconscious," my hero Jung, who late in his life was told in a dream that he had achieved "wholeness and singleness of self," wrote: "By *shadow* I mean the 'negative' side of the personality, the sum of all those unpleasant qualities we like to hide, together with the insufficiently developed functions and the content of the personal unconscious." This speaks to everyone, but especially to the great writer who was so guilt-ridden from all the betrayals and self-betrayals that he repressed to his unconscious that he created a monstrously vain, self-justifying, mean-spirited *shadow personality*.

At the risk of stepping off my precipice and inviting the kind of ridicule that flows so generously from incredulity, I have to offer my own experience of how impenetrable the fortress of our own vanity can be when it comes to the *shadow* side of our personality; and my literary mentor had immeasurably much more to be vain about than me. But I dealt with the issue of my vanity in my novel *Healing with Padre Pio*, so I can spare myself the indignity of repeating what blindness to my own vanity did to me; and because I dealt with the devastating issue of my vanity with the Ascended Master in my novel on spiritual healing, I have an uncanny insight into my literary mentor's *shadow* personality, or I would not dare to be so bold.

The young Hemingway was exceptionally talented, devilishly good looking (when he grew a moustache he looked like a young Clark Gable), always sporty and athletic, and naturally magnetic; but these qualities made him vain, and vanity makes one selfish and insensitive. And the more my mentor succeeded in his writing, the more critical and popular praise he received; and this fed his vanity and made him more selfish and insensitive, as his close friends began to see in his behavior towards his loving wife Hadley with the publication of *In Our Time*, and especially after the publication of *The Sun Also Rises* that launched his career into the literary stratosphere; but he tried to be the best person that he could be and repressed these unseemly qualities to the *shadow* side of his personality. But his *shadow* grew exponentially with every book that he wrote, and by the time he wrote *Across the River and into the Trees* that was inspired by his obsession with a young Venetian girl his *shadow* was powerful enough to break down the protective barriers of his mind and set the self-adulating and chaotic forces of the repressed unconscious side of his personality free, which can be seen in Lillian Ross's celebrated profile of the great author in the *New Yorker* shortly after writing the romantic fantasy that he vainly boasted to be the best novel of his career but which critics deemed to be his worst, but once set free by his wild romantic fantasy the chaotic forces of his *shadow* personality were channeled into *The Old Man and the Sea* that garnered him the Nobel Prize for Literature which gorged his wounded vanity and gave his *shadow* the power to take over his personality and force him to the Mayo Clinic for electroshock therapy; but this failed to cure him of his depression and paranoid delusions of persecution, and the great writer's great pride drove him to commit suicide because he had to live life on his own terms, or not at all.

"Martha Gellhorn, after reading the first installment of *Across the River and into the Trees,*" wrote Hemingway's insightful biographer, "was quick to conclude that her former husband doted only on himself. 'I feel sick,' she wrote Bill Walton, 'shivering sick.' She wept for the lost years she spent adoring him." To Martha, the story had "a long sound of madness and a terrible smell as of decay," concluded the biographer Michael Reynolds. And after she read the second of the five *Cosmopolitan* installments, she wrote Bill Walton that the book "was God's vengeance; but Ernest will never know. He will go on...always feeling misunderstood...always feeling everything is someone else's fault and I think...he will end up in the nut house" (*Hemingway the Final Years*, p. 223), and he probably would have needed psychiatric care had he not pre-empted the final indignity to his colossal vanity by blowing himself to hell with his favorite custom made shotgun.

It's ironic that Hemingway should have drawn the title of his novel on "the lost generation" that launched his writing career from the passage in *Ecclesiastes* that addresses the issue of vanity central to the *enantiodromiac* process of life that characterizes the dual nature of our evolving personality; because for all of his creative genius, the great writer failed to grasp the essential purpose of all his labor, which was to grow into the wholeness and singleness of self that he was meant to be: "*Vanity of vanities, saith the Preacher, vanity of vanities; all is vanity. What profit hath a man of all his labor which he taketh under the sun? One generation passeth away, and another generation cometh; but the earth abideth forever. The sun also riseth, and the sun goeth down, and hasteth to the place where he arose...*" (Eccl. 1: 2-5)—the very same passage that inspired my royal edict of self-denial and changed the course of my life; the critical difference being that my mentor got swallowed up by his lion, while I ended up swallowing mine.

18. When Life Is Not Enough

It happened in my second year at university where I had been called to study philosophy to help find my true self, philosophy being the "mother of all disciplines" and the logical discipline to study; but in the second semester of my second year I began to feel that I had been cast adrift in a sea of endless speculation, and I began to panic; and one weekend I drove home and went for one of my philosopher's walks down the railroad tracks behind our house to the man-made breakwater and little "island" in the middle of the Nipigon River.

It may not be relevant, but I think it is relevant on a very deep level where something always affects me long before I become aware of it consciously, but I had a philosophy professor who made such a strong impression upon me that I dreaded ending up like him at the end of my philosophy studies.

He was Dr. Doan, a life-long bachelor who wore starched white shirts and always had a cigarette in his nicotine-stained fingers when he wasn't lecturing. He taught Metaphysics and Aesthetics, and he was deemed to be the wise man on campus; but the impression I got was that he was the loneliest man in the world.

I often saw him standing in the window of his office high up in the Ryan Building smoking a cigarette and staring out into the world, as though waiting for something to happen. I don't know what he was waiting for, but every time I saw him whenever I drove into the campus I felt a sudden pang of sorrow for my professor, and I said to myself, "Is that what philosophy leads to?"

And then one day he gave us an assignment which would count instead of our final term paper. We were to keep a journal and record our dreams and reflections and hand it in so he could mark us on our private thoughts, which he deemed would be our most philosophical but which I could not honor because I felt it invasive, if not perverse; and I went to his office to explain my reason why.

"I've always kept a journal, and I don't know if I'm comfortable having someone read my private thoughts. I'd rather write a term paper," I said; and knowing better to not argue the point, he assigned me a topic. But when I got my paper back it was full of red marks and all kinds of comments that I found irrelevant to my paper; and I knew that philosophy had served its purpose for me.

On my lonely walk to the little "island" in the middle of the river that was connected to the mainland by the man-made stone breakwater that divided the Nipigon River to create a bay for our little marina, I thought about my life and what I was going to do; because regardless how hard I tried to justify my reasons for studying philosophy, I could not suppress the feeling that I had been cast adrift in a sea of endless philosophical speculation; and I had to get back to *terra firma*.

I was always intimidated by great thinkers, and I had sycophantic respect for great minds like Bertrand Russell, Jean-Paul Sartre, Nietzsche, and Albert Camus; but the more I studied philosophy, the more I began to feel that they were only guessing—albeit, with a brilliance that masked the core of their philosophical doubt; and as I walked to the little "island" where I sat and smoked half a dozen cigarettes as I pondered what to do, I realized that I could not trust philosophy to bring me to where I wanted to go, so I got up and headed back home. But I stopped about twenty feet from the mainland and looked up into the sky; and with my heart in my throat, I said: "Dear God, I know that we get nothing for nothing in this world, or any world for that matter; so please tell me, what price truth?"

I knew that there was a price to pay for what I sought, but I was willing to pay whatever was asked of me; and then my attention turned to the river as it rushed past me in swift currents on its way to mighty Lake Superior, and for some reason I thought of *Ecclesiastes* and recited from heart the same passage that inspired the title of Hemingway's first novel; and when I recited the verse *"All the rivers run into the sea, yet the sea is not full; unto the place from whence the rivers come, thither they return again"* I got a stirring in my soul that I had to go to the source of my life to find my true self. And then the play *Oedipus Rex* came to mind, and in my mind's eye I saw King Oedipus blind and broken from the knowledge that his soothsayer Tiresias had given him that he was responsible for the plague that had befallen his kingdom, and true to the edict that he had imposed that whoever was responsible for the plague would be banished from Thebes, Oedipus gouged out his eyes for his heinous crime of patricide and defiling his mother's bed and banished himself out of his own kingdom; and in a moment of what I'd like to believe was divine inspiration, I knew exactly what price I had to pay for the truth I sought: *I had to banish myself out of the kingdom of my own senses.* And I took out my little notebook from my jacket pocket and jotted down my edict of self-denial that I came to call my *Royal Dictum,* which I vowed to keep for the rest of my life; and the moment I stepped off the breakwater and onto the mainland I threw my cigarettes away and began my long and painful journey out of the private kingdom of my own senses.

For three and a half years I denied myself every pleasure of my life, which I could not have done without Gurdjieff's techniques of *self-remembering* and *non-identifying*; but one evening I was sitting in the lonely comfort of my separate apartment that we had built attached to our family home, and I got the strongest urge to read *Ecclesiastes* again; and when I came to the closing verses, I heard the call again so loud and clear that I knew what I had to do: *"And further, by these, my son, be admonished: of making many books there is no end; and much study is a weariness of the flesh. Let us hear the conclusion of the whole matter: Fear God, and keep his commandments: for this is the whole duty of man. For God shall bring every work into judgment, whether it be good, or whether it be evil."* I shut my Bible and showered and changed clothes and went to a local bar and joined three young ladies and ordered a drink for them and scotch and water for myself, and by the end of the evening I asked one of the young ladies if I could take her home; but we went to my apartment instead and made love, thus ending my royal edict of self-denial.

In those three and a half bittersweet years I initiated myself into the mysteries of "the way of the sly man," and I learned how to "catch" the subtle life force that I needed to grow into the person that I was meant to be, because the more I denied myself the pleasures of life the more I learned how to "store my treasures in heaven," thereby breaking the code of Christ's cryptic sayings; but I need not expound upon this here because I've done so in my novel *Jesus Wears Dockers*.

In my self-denial I learned what Gurdjieff meant when he said that nature can only evolve us so far and no further, and to evolve into the person that we are meant to be we have to take evolution into our own hands; which I did with Gurdjieff's teaching, my *Royal Dictum*, and the sayings of Jesus, and one fine day I experienced the birth of my immortal self in my mother's kitchen while she was kneading bread dough on the kitchen table, thus ending my lonely quest for my true self.

So when I read what Katherine Mansfield said about literature not being enough, I *knew* what she meant and applauded her reason for seeking Gurdjieff out; she needed a teaching that would complete her life, because literature had brought her as far as it could take her and she had to find a way to satisfy the desperate longing in her soul for completeness and wholeness of self.

That's why I've always felt an underlying sense of despair in Hemingway's writing; but when the movie *Hemingway and Gellhorn* opened me up to the *enantiodromiac* principle of life, I knew I had to go back to Hemingway and read him with fresh eyes—because the movie made me see that his whole life told the story of man's mythic journey to his true self; and despite the fact that his heroic life ended in tragic suicide, I finally understood the reason why.

19. Hemingway's Literary Experiment

What became painfully obvious to me upon my return to Hemingway as I began to read him with fresh eyes (along with all the new biographies that I had ordered) was just how much of his life went into his stories; so much, in fact, that I doubt that any one of his stories came straight from his imagination.

I don't think any did, because if he began his stories with one true sentence it had to come from life experience; and he built the rest of his story upon the reality of his one true sentence, blending the reality of his experience with the reality of his imagination; and the result made him a famous writer. But then he tried something different: he wrote a story straight out of personal experience, drawn from a big game hunting safari, which he called *Green Hills of Africa*; and here's what he said about his literary experiment by way of introduction:

"Unlike many novels, none of the characters or incidents in this book is imaginary. Any one not finding sufficient love interest is at liberty, while reading it, to insert whatever love interest he or she may have at the time. The writer has attempted to write an absolutely true book to see whether the shape of a country and the pattern of a month's action can, if truly presented, compete with a work of imagination."

It couldn't compete, and *Green Hills of Africa* failed to satisfy that longing readers have for that certain *je ne sais quoi* that comes with stories inspired by the author's imagination; and my mentor learned an invaluable lesson that he passed on to writers who want to learn the secrets of creative writing.

Like everyone else, my mentor had no idea what imagination adds to a story; and the most that he could say was that it was like the dust on a butterfly's wings. All very nice and poetic, but it added nothing to our understanding of the power of imagination to transform reality into a deeper perception of what is.

But when he got over licking his wounds from what the critics had to say about *Green Hills of Africa*, he tapped into his creative genius once more and used the same experience to write two of the best short stories of his writing career and all of literature—"The Short Happy Life of Francis Macomber" and "The Snows of Kilimanjaro," proving to himself and to the world that a work of straight memoir simply cannot compete with a good work of the imagination.

But what the hell is this thing called imagination, anyway? What is this miraculous power that can turn dull facts into the truth above the facts of life that we call art? Is that why *Green Hills of Africa* failed to compete with a work of the imagination, because Hemingway never got to the truth above the facts of his safari experience, however exciting he tried to make it with his enormous talent but which he did with his two short stories that were inspired by the same safari?

Is this why readers prefer good novels over memoirs? My hero Jung never trusted memoirs, and I can understand why; but he went on to write one of the most read and loved memoirs in the world, *Memories, Dreams, Reflections*, which I've read at least three times and delved into dozens of times because Jung's insights into his inner life continued to enlighten mine. And my other hero wrote his own enlightening memoir that came to be called *A Moveable Feast* (a beautiful title that A. E. Hotchner was responsible for, which he suggested to Mary Hemingway when he found the descriptive phrase in one of Hemingway's letters), and it has become one of Hemingway's most loved books. In fact, so poignant was his memoir that it inspired *Paris without End, The True Story of Hemingway's First Wife*, by Gioia Diliberto, a novel *The Paris Wife* by Paula McLain, and *The Paris Pilgrims*, an underappreciated novel by Clancy Carlile that throws a whole new light on the great writer's apprenticeship that he wrote about in *A Moveable Feast*.

Memoirs can be fascinating, and very enjoyable to read (personally, I love reading memoirs and biographies; but like Jung, I've grown to distrust them and have to be very careful about what to believe); and not unlike Francisco Goldman who wrote his novel *Say Her Name* based on his marriage to Aura Estrada, I too have come to believe that a writer has to make up his story to get to the truth of his story; that's why Goldman preferred to write a novel instead of a memoir.

Hemingway wrote *Islands in the Stream* to get closer to the truth of his life and wives and children; and he wrote *The Garden of Eden* to get to the deeper, more hidden truth of his very private and androgynous sex life; that's why his straight memoir *Green Hills of Africa* failed to compete with a work of the imagination where his short stories inspired by the same safari succeeded so well that they will be studied by students of literature for generations to come. So again, what is it about imagination that has the power to transform the dry facts of life into art?

It's ironic, but the movie *Hemingway and Gellhorn* that sent me back to my high school hero and opened a window onto the *enantiodromiac* principle that drives the individuation process of our self-becoming also provided an answer to this question of the miraculous power of imagination; but I would never have resolved the mystery had I not experienced it in my own creative writing first.

Like Hemingway and every other writer, I never understood how imagination worked; all I knew was that it was indispensable to the creative process. And as Hemingway found out only too sadly as the critics skewered *Green Hills of Africa* (mainly because he skewered them in his story), he needed the miraculous power of imagination to transform the facts of his life into art; and this power that transforms the facts of our life into art is the inherently self-transcending power of the *transcendent function* that is activated by the creative process.

Here I am once again then, standing on the edge of my precipice; and the only way to make sense of what I have learned about the miraculous power of imagination is to jump off and hope for the best. But I have precedent for what I'm going to do, which will make my leap of faith less risky; and that's to offer an insight into the mysterious power of the creative process by way of personal analogy. So, if I may; let me offer an experience that I had that will help to explain the principle of *enantiodromia* at the heart of life, an experience that I had when I was a runner.

In my thirties I was nudged by my inner guidance to take up running, and when I'm strongly nudged to do something I usually do (or suffer the consequences because it means having to learn my lessons the hard way); so I bought all the books that I could find on running and the proper attire and my first pair of good running shoes, appropriately called *New Balance*, in a store in Winnipeg called Pheidippides (named after the ancient Greek who ran the first marathon), and I started running.

Actually I didn't start running for two or three weeks; every day I jogged a short distance first, then walked, then jogged, then walked and jogged and so on until I built up my aerobic capacity and running legs, and I did this in the privacy of deserted bush roads on the outskirts of my hometown of Nipigon, in Northwestern Ontario where no one could see my labored efforts to become the runner I wanted to be. And when I could jog without having to stop to walk I quickened my pace and ran on the highway along the shoreline of Lake Helen, which was where I ran in my dream experience that revealed the *enantiodromiac* power of self-becoming.

By this time I was hooked on running and ran seven miles every day after my day's work of contract painting, and I was also living "the way of the sly man" that I had learned to master with Gurdjieff's teaching, and every morning before going to work I recited three times a long list of principles to live by during the day so I could mold my life into the ideal that I sought to be, which was inspired by Wordsworth's poem "Character of the Happy Warrior."

Every morning before going to work I recited all those principles that I had strung together from all my reading and life experiences to mold my character into my Wordsworthian ideal, always laboring "good on good to fix" and trying to be the best person that I could be, which I did for years; and then I had my running dream that revealed the miraculous power of the *enantiodromiac* principle of self-becoming that is central to the natural individuation process of our identity.

In my dream I begin my run down the same highway along the shoreline of Lake Helen in front of St. Sylvester's Historic Mission Church where I had volunteered six weeks of my time to paint and decorate (and store precious treasures in heaven with my charity) and where I always began my daily run, and it's a beautiful sunny day for a long distance run; but as I'm running down the highway I have a ball of string in my mouth and an invisible hand in front of me pulling the string out of my mouth as I run, and the further I run the smaller the ball of string becomes, and it gets smaller, and smaller, and smaller; and I wake up.

The ball of string in my mouth was made up of many small pieces of string tied together and rolled up into a ball, and it took a few days to decode the message of my dream; but when I did I was amazed at the miraculous power of the unconscious to create an image so perfect in understanding that it gave me a whole new respect for my hero C. G. Jung who said in *The Red Book*, "My dreams are the speech of my soul...Dreams are the guiding words of the soul. They pave the way for life, and they determine you without understanding their language," which confirmed what America's greatest psychic Edgar Cayce had to say about dreams: "They work to accomplish two things. They work to solve the problems of the dreamer's conscious, waking life. And they work to quicken in the dreamer new potentials which are his to claim" (*Edgar Cayce on Dreams*, by Harmon N. Bro, PhD under the editorship of Hugh Lynn Cayce).

Although I had not yet become acquainted with the Jungian concept of *enantiodromia*, which would take many more years to prepare me for (as I've firmly come to believe, our life really *is* choreographed; and we only get what we need to know at the time we need to know it, and not before), my running dream revealed the mechanics of the *enantiodromiac* principle at work in my life, thereby resolving for me the strange comment made by Dr. George Sheehan, who was called "the guru of running" and whose book *Running & Being: The Total Experience* I had read; he said, "In running I found my salvation," which puzzled everyone but other runners who had also experienced the salvific joy of running but who could not explain what it meant either; but because of the serendipitous coupling of my two experiences (1, reciting my principles every morning; and 2, distance running), the genius of my creative unconscious gave me a dream that revealed the secret of the *enantiodromiac* principle, which was the mystery of self-becoming; or, if you will, the natural way of how we grow ontologically in the consciousness of our own identity.

Here's how my dream revealed this mystery to me: The ball of string in my mouth is made up of tiny pieces of string all strung together and rolled up into a little ball in my mouth, and it is being pulled out of my mouth as I'm running. Each piece of string symbolizes one of the principles that I "mouthed" every morning before I went to work to remind myself to live by that principle so I could realize my ideal self. Jesus said that one has to *do* his sayings for them to work in their life; that's the only way one can build his house upon a rock. *Doing* is the operative word, and as I went out into the marketplace and lived my principles I "walked my talk," as the saying goes. I *lived* what I "mouthed" every morning, which in my dream was symbolized by the ball of string being pulled out of my mouth as I ran.

Running symbolizes *doing*, or living my principles; and the further I ran, the more I *lived* my principles—but the ball of string got smaller, and smaller, and smaller; and this meant that I was ontologically *becoming* the principles that I "mouthed" every morning. Or, to express this less abstrusely; in the *doing*, I was growing in the consciousness of what I was *doing*—i. e., I was growing in the consciousness of the principles that I was living; and my dream was telling me that running activated the *enantiodromiac* principle of self-becoming. This is why Dr. George Sheehan found his salvation in running, because running activated the *enantiodromiac* principle of his self-becoming and he grew in wholeness and singleness of self every time he went for a run, thereby fulfilling his destiny of becoming the person that he was meant to be—ergo, his puzzling comment "In running I found my salvation!"

I understood Dr. Sheehan's comment, because I also experienced the salvific joy of running every time I went for a run; but I did not understand what that meant until I had my running dream experience. And once I had the experience of the *enantiodromiac* principle fixed as a dream image in my mind (dream images are what Jung called "the speech of my soul"), I recognized it as the fundamental principle of the natural individuation process of life; and it would only be a matter of time before I conceptualized it in my writing, which I did with every new book that I wrote until I was ready to see that *enantiodromia* was the central principle of all creative writing; which was why I felt compelled to watch *Hemingway and Gellhorn*, because this movie would awaken me to the natural principle of self-becoming in my high school hero's paradoxical life, and this in turn would awaken me to the redemptive power of self-becoming that is activated by the power of imagination central to the process of creative writing, and all the arts.

In Jungian terms, imagination activates the *transcendent function*, which resolves the *enantiodromiac* principle of our self-becoming; and the *transcendent function* can be activated simply by *doing*—because in the *doing*, we *become*, especially concentrated and disciplined *doing* like running or creative writing; and *becoming* is the purpose of life. But—and this is the BUT of all buts—this kind of natural doing will only take us so far in our self-becoming; or, as Gurdjieff said, nature will only evolve us so far, and no further. This is why my high school hero could never realize his destiny of wholeness and singleness of self, because the *transcendent function* of his becoming that he activated with writing was not enough to liberate him from the prison of his *non-being*, or *shadow* self. Unlike Dr. George Sheehan who found salvation in his daily runs, Hemingway found salvation in his daily writing; but it was not enough to save him from himself.

The tragic irony of Hemingway's life was that he was aware of his own *transcendent function*, which is why he loved to write more than anything else that he loved to do, including marlin fishing in the Gulf Stream which gave him enormous pleasure and satisfaction, because writing opened him up to the inherently self-transcending power of his imagination as it did in his favorite story "The Short Happy Life of Francis Macomber." In this brilliant story of redemption, the cowardly husband salvaged the dignity that he had forfeited to his overbearing wife; and as short-lived as his salvation was, he died happy.

Holding on to his dignity was Hemingway's life-long struggle, which he severely damaged when he betrayed his first wife Hadley by having an affair with Pauline Pfeiffer, who undoubtedly went into his model for Macomber's bitchy wife; and he idealized his own *enantiodromiac* struggle in the fictional life of Francis Macomber. That's why a memoir and "absolutely true book" like *Green Hills of Africa* could never compete with a work of the imagination like "The Short Happy Life of Francis Macomber"—because creative writing activates the *transcendent function* of self-becoming that satisfies the longing in our soul to be our true self.

Hemingway wasn't consciously aware of it, but his literary experiment with *Green Hills of Africa* proved that he needed the power of imagination to satisfy the longing in his soul to be all that he could be, which he ironically symbolized in his intensely autobiographical story "The Snows of Kilimanjaro" by revealing how his dying protagonist Harry could have become more than what he was had he not betrayed himself by compromising his talent for the easy life that the wealthy women that he married provided for him. Without being aware that creative writing activated the *transcendent function* of self-becoming, Hemingway was growing into all that he could be through the power of his imagination in the stories that he wrote; that's why he loved to write more than anything else that he loved to do. But, sadly, it wasn't enough to save him from himself; and he died a tragic hero.

20. The Portrait in Hemingway's Attic

"Memoir is the facts of life. Fiction is the truth of life," said Alice Munroe to Shelagh Rogers on her CBC show *The Next Chapter* shortly after Munroe was awarded the 2013 Nobel Prize for Literature "for her mastery of the contemporary short story," which moved me enough to make a commitment to read one Munroe story every week out of respect for our first Canadian writer to be awarded the most prestigious prize in literature; and I began with the title story of her book *The Love of a Good Woman*. But because I had come back to Hemingway, starting with his short stories, the mystique of Munroe's stories revealed itself to me, and I never enjoyed her stories more; so I was thankful again for watching the movie *Hemingway and Gellhorn* that brought me back to my high school hero, because it gave me a whole new love, respect, and appreciation for great literature.

After rereading a goodly number of Hemingway's short stories and Carlos Baker's *Hemingway: The Writer as Artist* (I had already read Baker's door-stopping authorized biography *Ernest Hemingway: A Life Story*, but I delved into it again here and there just to refresh my memory), I felt inclined to read about my mentor's youth, so I took out my book *Ernest Hemingway, The Early Years* by Charles A. Fenton and devoured it again in a few sittings. And this inspired me to read for the first time a book that I kept meaning to read but never did, a novel called *The Paris Pilgrims*, by Clancy Carlile; and it proved to be so insightful on the mind and manners and early influences on Hemingway's life that I berated myself for not reading it sooner—because *The Paris Pilgrims* was much more revealing than the biography I had just read of Hemingway's early years in Paris, and for me it was proof positive of what Alice Munroe meant about fiction being the truth of life.

In other words, if *A Moveable Feast* was the *facts* of Hemingway's Parisian life (as he remembered it), then *The Paris Pilgrims* was the *truth* of Hemingway's Parisian life. Of course, the novel was fiction; but so rich in biographical detail was it (which I knew was accurate from all the reading that I had done) that it painted a portrait of the young Hemingway that rang so true for me that it automatically brought to mind Oscar Wilde's devilishly brilliant novel *The Picture of Dorian Grey*; and reading *The Paris Pilgrims* felt like I had been given the rare privilege of stepping into Hemingway's attic and looking at the early stages of the evolving portraiture of his blemishing soul, which gave me a much deeper understanding of my high school hero and literary mentor.

Dorian Gray was a wealthy, cultured, and devastatingly beautiful young man who captured Basil Hallward's artistic imagination, and Basil painted several portraits of him, depicting Dorian as an ancient Greek hero and mythological figure; but Dorian realized that as he grew older and infirm his portrait would always remind him of the beauty he will have lost, and in a fit of overpowering distress he cursed his portrait and cravenly pledged his soul if only he could stay young forever and have his portrait bear the burden of his aging life and infamy.

Dorian then fell under the influence of the nefarious Lord Henry Wotton, who celebrated youth, beauty, and the selfish pursuit of pleasure; and Dorian's first betrayal of love, for the actress Sibyl Vane who commits suicide when Dorian breaks off his engagement with her, appears as a blemish on the face of his portrait; and realizing that his sins will now appear on the face of his portrait, Dorian hides it in an upper room of his house where no one else but he can see it.

As Dorian abandons to a life of hedonistic pleasure, every sin and betrayal that he commits is recorded in his portrait in the attic; but he remains forever young and beautiful. Then one day he shows his hideous portrait to the artist Basil, who is so horrified that he begs Dorian to repent; but Dorian cannot, and in a fit of rage stabs the artist and kills him. Wracked by fear and guilt, Dorian resolves to amend his life, but he cannot muster the courage to confess his crimes and his portrait reveals the hypocrisy of his repentance with a sneer; and in a fit of fury Dorian picks up the knife that he used to kill the artist and stabs his portrait to destroy it. There is a crash, and Dorian's servants enter to find the portrait unharmed, showing Dorian as a beautiful young man, and on the floor lies the body of their master, horribly wrinkled and disfigured with a knife plunged into its heart.

The genius of Oscar Wilde to capture the dark *shadow* side of our personality in the metaphor of Dorian Gray's hidden portrait in the attic goes a long way to explaining Hemingway's paradoxical personality, and it wouldn't be a stretch by any means to draw comparisons between Hemingway and Dorian Gray.

Dorian's portrait began to change with the betrayal of his love for Sibyl, and by all accounts (especially by Hemingway himself in *A Moveable Feast*), the portrait in Hemingway's attic showed its first hideous blemish when he betrayed his love for Hadley by having an affair with the fashionable and wealthy Pauline Pfeiffer; a blemish on his soul that he could never resolve and which haunted him to the end of his life but which he finally owned up to in his confessional memoir.

Love is our most sacred gift, and nothing can damage our soul more than when we betray love; and at the risk of stepping off my precipice and inviting the ridicule of incredulity, I know that we carry the guilt of our betrayal of love from one lifetime to the next, as I did when I betrayed my love for Penny in our past life together in Genoa, Italy. I wrote about this in my novel *Cathedral of My Past Lives*, so I need not expound upon it here; but I know from painful experience that one's karmic debt to love has to be paid back, which is why Penny and I are together again.

It doesn't surprise me then that Hemingway felt the way he did when he reflected back on his life in *A Moveable Feast*; he realized the enormity of the betrayal of his love for Hadley, because the damage it did to his soul set a dangerous pattern of betrayal for the rest of his life; and every time he betrayed his wives and friends and personal conscience it was recorded in the portrait in his attic.

Of course, the portrait in Hemingway's attic is a metaphor for the dark *shadow* side of his larger-than-life personality, which by the end of his life became so burdened by the insufferable guilt of all his betrayals that he felt compelled to destroy himself just as Dorian Gray felt compelled to destroy his hideous portrait; and as tragic as it was, my high school hero had no one to blame but himself because this was the bargain that he had made with himself to become the great writer that he always wanted to be; and the moral of Ernest Hemingway's life, as he revealed in his wistful memoir, is that whatever success we achieve in life it's not worth the price when we betray love, and *"I wish I would have died before I loved anyone but her"* will go down in history as one of the saddest lines in all of literature.

21. A Full Spectrum of Emotions

Paul Hendrickson wrote something very insightful about Ernest Hemingway in his superlative National Book Critics Award-winning book *Hemingway's Boat, Everything He Loved in Life and Lost, 1934-1961* that speaks to the effect the great writer has on everyone who reads him: "I also believe that all of Hemingway's writing, every bit of it, even at its most self-parodistic and Papa-cult worst, is seeking to be about the *living* of this life. The being of this life. The doing of this life. And in that sense, the work—and even, I am willing to say, so much of the coarsened personal history—can be thought of as something spiritual and indeed almost holy," which was why even in his suicide I felt a certain grace; but why? Why does Hemingway have this effect on his readers? What grace can there be in suicide?

This speaks to the mystique of literature, with which I'm familiar enough through all of my reading and writing to offer an informed perspective, and which coupled with the hard-won wisdom of my quest for my true self may just open a window onto the aura of the holy in Hemingway's writing, and all of literature; and yes, even his suicide. But once again, I have to take a giant leap of faith.

"Literature is not enough," said Katherine Mansfield, and every disillusioned writer that has been brought to the limits of what literature can do to satisfy that longing in our soul but leaves one desperately wanting; but literature being a deeper perception of life, it follows that life is not enough to satisfy that longing in our soul for wholeness and singleness of self; which goes a long way to explaining the underlying sadness that flows through all of literature, and most especially in Hemingway's writing whose basic theme was all about the struggle.

Metaphorically speaking, which is the most effective way for literature to convey the truth above the facts of life, literature is like a spiritual diet that we can enjoy every day of our life, like reading a poem every morning before taking on our daily struggles, but which cannot provide us with all the nutrients necessary (or not enough, as Mansfield sadly realized) to satisfy that longing in our soul for our true self; that's why so many disillusioned writers and artists become seekers.

I was a seeker before I became a writer, and I learned how to "catch" enough of the vital life force to grow into my true self (confirming the Sufi saying that "spirituality cannot be taught, but must be caught"); so I have a gnostic awareness of what it takes to satisfy that longing in our soul, and I agree with Hendrickson that Hemingway's writing was all about *living* this life—because Hemingway had to get the most out of this life to satisfy his voracious hunger to become the great writer that he wanted to be; and his enormous appetite for life brought out the best and worst in him and gave him a full spectrum of emotions that made him one of the most engaging existential writers of modern literature.

Every biographer that has delved into Hemingway's life (and he's had a few) had to deal with the issue of his paradoxical personality; and although bipolarism and "black-ass" depression go a long way to explaining his volatile behavior, the question is left open as to why he could be so kind and sensitive and understanding one day and so cruel and vicious and abusive the next—or, as he demonstrated in the last decade of his life, not from day to day but from one moment to the next; a volatile personality that even tried the patience of his closest and most forgiving friend General Buck Lanham with the way he publically humiliated his wife Mary when she had worked so hard to arrange the lavish party to celebrate her husband's sixtieth birthday at their friend's villa in Spain, and for which Lanham could never bring himself to forgive his friend despite Hemingway's apologies.

125

Hemingway was unpredictable, and his mood swings could be switched on by the smallest thing, especially when he was drinking which was practically every day, and his capricious behavior exasperated everyone around him; but he couldn't help himself, because like every *shadow*-afflicted individual Hemingway was his own worst enemy, and this is the key of Hemingway's bedeviled personality.

Here we go again, then; into the breach of incredulity as I try to explain how our teleologically-driven need for self-identity creates the *shadow* side of our personality with every life that we live and which we take with us as karmic baggage from one life to the next until the natural process of individuation can take us no further and we have to take evolution into our own hands to break the endless cycle of karma and reincarnation but are stopped dead in our tracks by the dilemma of our paradoxical nature like my high school hero Ernest Hemingway.

The premise of this mischievous esoteric perspective is that we live more than one lifetime, which for me is not philosophy or speculation; and the purpose of every life that we live is to grow in the consciousness of our own being until we realize our true self. In a letter to "Anonymous", dated July 10, 1946, Carl Jung counseled a person from this very same perspective in an effort to talk them out of committing suicide: "The idea of suicide, understandable as it is, does not seem commendable to me. *We live to attain the greatest possible amount of spiritual development and self-awareness.* As long as life is possible, even if only in a minimal degree, you should hang on to it, in order to scoop it up for the purpose of conscious development" (*Selected Letters of G. G. Jung, 1909-1961.* Italics mine).

"Scooping" up life then is the key to realizing our own identity. This is why Martha Gellhorn could not stay married to Ernest Hemingway, because his domineering personality stifled her growth and she had to leave him to "scoop" up life and grow in her own identity. Which is precisely what made Hemingway such a cruel and miserable bastard, because he fed off other people's energy to grow in his own identity; especially his four wives who were no match for his alpha personality.

This is a primordial thing, and had I not been regressed to my first primordial human lifetime where I was the dominant alpha male of a group of higher primates that appropriated their will-to-be with power grunts and savage beatings until I constellated enough life force to give birth to the "I" of my own identity, I would never have come to understand the subtle exchange of energies that goes on between people; and my high school hero Ernest Hemingway proved himself to be a very conscious and highly evolved alpha male personality who drew upon the vital energy of other people with his charisma and animal magnetism and winning boyish charm and brilliant intellect and natural learning skills and prodigious memory and intimate knowledge of everything that he took an interest in like bullfighting and big game hunting and deep sea fishing and a very competitive spirit that hated to lose (his loss in the boxing ring to the much smaller Morley Callaghan, which he blamed on his friend Scott Fitzgerald for not ringing the bell in time, has become legendary); and like all alpha males he could be vicious, cruel, and downright mean whenever he didn't get what he wanted to satisfy his voracious hunger to be. And the more Ernest "Papa" Hemingway grew into his own identity as the great writer, the more energy he had to have to feed the appetite of his insatiable ego-personality. That's how he created the monstrous *shadow* side of his personality that had enough power to take control of his ego and wreak havoc in his life, especially when he was drinking; but I had to see the movie *Hemingway and Gellhorn* to become aware of this primordial dynamic in my high school hero's predatory personality.

That's why I exclaimed, *"He had to be a prick to become the great writer that he became!"* The movie had awakened me to the *enantiodromiac* principle of the great writer's life, how the constant play of his dark *shadow* side and conscious ego-personality generated the emotional sparks that nurtured his identity and gave him new energy for his writing—not unlike

Wagner who it was said intentionally created heated arguments and then dashed off and poured his emotional energy into his compositions; but it was not a healthy thing to do, because instead of transcending himself Hemingway's selfish *shadow* kept him trapped in a vicious cycle of self-destruction, which his last three contentious marriages attested to. This was why I was directed by my inner guidance to part company with my high school hero and blaze my own trail through life, because as he was born to become a great writer I was born to find my true self; and to do that I had to find a path that would set me free from the karmically-burdened *shadow* side of my ego-personality.

I found my path in Gurdjieff's teaching, which opened me up to the eminent psychologist who believed that one-sidedness in one's conscious attitude begets an unconscious reaction, which Jung defined as the *enantiodromiac* principle. *Enantiodromia* literally means "running counter to," and Jung saw this Yin and Yang dynamic as the emergence of the unconscious opposite in the course of time which occurs when an extreme one-sided tendency dominates conscious life but in time an equally powerful counter position is built up that inhibits conscious performance and subsequently breaks through the conscious control, as the unconscious *shadow* side of Hemingway's massive ego-personality had a greater and greater capacity to do as he grew in mythic stature.

"If we listen to our unconscious, it will help us to avoid exaggeration; it will help us to find our center, our true self," said Jung. "One must be what one is. One must discover one's own individuality, that center of personality, which is equidistant between the conscious and the unconscious; we must aim for that ideal point towards which nature appears to be directing us"—which Hemingway tried to do with every story and novel that he wrote, because writing was his moral compass; but he could never find that equidistant point between his conscious ego-personality and his dark *shadow* side, losing more and more ground to his *shadow* self as he got older, and this never-ending Sisyphean struggle was the tragedy of his life.

Hemingway was a man of extremes; when he did something he jumped in with both feet. And because he was such a phenomenally quick study, he picked up things so rapidly that he became an expert practically overnight on whatever grabbed his interest; like bullfighting. Something about bullfighting touched the very core of his artistic being, because the first time he witnessed the drama of the lone matador and wild and untamed bull he saw the whole wisdom of *Ecclesiastes* in the spectacle, which became the central metaphor of his novel *The Sun Also Rises* that magnified the vanity of life in "the lost generation" and launched his writing career.

In all honesty, I had no idea why I HAD to watch the movie *Hemingway and Gellhorn;* and not until I intuited the *enantiodromiac* principle (which I had not yet conceptualized) at play in his contentious relationship with his wife Martha did I begin to understand my life-long fascination for my high school hero.

Ernest Hemingway symbolized the culmination of the natural process of individuation, and he was marked for tragedy because he tried to satisfy the inherent longing in his soul for wholeness and singleness of self through life experience; but despite his remarkable effort to satisfy his longing with every new experience that he embraced with all the passion of his being, life always left him wanting. That's what made him a Sisyphean hero doomed to repeat his life over, and over, and over again but never getting to the promised land of his true self—because, as my enlightened hero Jung had come to see, to complete what nature leaves unfinished we have to take evolution into our own hands; and this is where I have to take another leap of faith and open the door to the mystery of our becoming.

Hemingway speaks to the precarious reality of our existential life; but if, as I have come to believe, we live more than one lifetime, and if, as I have come to believe, we are all immortal souls born to realize our spiritual nature, and if, as I have also come to believe, we cannot do this on our own and need help from someone who has realized their spiritual nature, someone like Socrates whose philosophy guides us out of the cave of shadows and reflections to the light of our true self, then one has to step out of the existential paradigm so brilliantly captured in Hemingway's writing but which keeps one trapped in a literature that can never be enough to satisfy the longing in our soul for wholeness and singleness of self and look at life from a new perspective outside the existential paradigm of one lifetime, a perspective of karma and reincarnation, because that's the only way we can make sense of the absurd and meaningless fate of man's Sisyphean struggle. We have to know why the leopard on Mt. Kilimanjaro never found its way into the House of God; because for all of his creative genius, Hemingway couldn't tell us.

22. Hemingway's Reason for Living

"Suppose," said Katherine Mansfield to her mentor, "that I could succeed in writing as well as Shakespeare. It would be lovely, but what then? There is something wanting in literary art even at its highest. Literature is not enough. The greatest literature is still only mere literature if it has not a purpose commensurate with its art. Presence or absence of purpose distinguishes literature from mere literature, and the elevation of the purpose distinguishes literature within literature. That is merely literary that has no other object than to please. Minor literature has a didactic object. But the greatest literature of all—the literature that scarcely exists—has not merely an aesthetic object, nor merely a didactic object, but, in addition, a creative object; that of subjecting its readers to a real and at the same time illuminating experience. Major literature, in short, is an initiation into truth."

"But where do we stand in relation to that?" asks Orage.

"Where is the writer with the keys of initiation upon him?" replies Katherine Mansfield, concluding that one must become more to write better. (*A. R. Orage On Love, With Some Aphorisms & Other Essays*, Samuel Weiser, pp. 38-9).

This is why Hemingway called Mansfield's stories near-beer, because her stories lacked what the great writer had come to realize went into major literature, the literature that initiates one into the truth of life. This explains why Hemingway was so driven to experience all the life that he could, because with every experience he had he initiated himself deeper into the truth of life which he then wrote about; which explains his obsessive fascination with bullfighting, because in the spectacle of the bullfight he witnessed the whole symbolic drama of man's relationship with life—the pursuit of excellence, the struggle, and inevitable death.

But, to his undying sorrow, life just wasn't enough to satisfy the longing in his soul to realize the fullness of his being; and, ironically, this was why Katherine Mansfield sought Gurdjieff out; she was looking for the key to initiate herself into the deepest truth of life which literature could not provide. But after living at Gurdjieff's Institute for a few months she had grown enough to look at literature with a new perspective, which she shared with Orage just before she died.

After much reflection in the loft of the cowshed where she spent the last days of her life because Gurdjieff wanted her to breathe in the air of the cowshed for the good of her fragile health, she came to realize that a writer sees life like a camera, and to write major literature she had to not only widen the scope of her camera but write her new stories with a creative attitude towards life.

"What I am trying to say," she explained to Orage, "is that a new attitude to life on the part of writers would first see life different, and then make it different," which speaks to the *transcendent function* of the creative process that my high school hero illustrated with artistic genius in the two short stories inspired by the same safari experience that he used to write *Green Hills of Africa*—"The Short Happy Life of Francis Macomber," and "The Snows of Kilimanjaro."

In both of these stories he drew upon the dry facts of his safari experience, but by inseminating these facts with his imagination he *created* two stories that initiated him (and the reader) into a deeper perception of the way it could have been; or, into a deeper truth of life that was born of his imagination and safari experience. In these stories he created a whole new reality of possibility; and by doing so he transcended the facts of life and gave birth to a deeper perception of the truth of life.

"I was dying of poverty of life," Katherine Mansfield wrote to her husband John Middleton Murry from the Priory (Gurdjieff's Institute) in Fontainebleau-Avon. "In the deepest sense I've always been disunited. And this which has been my 'secret sorrow' has become everything for me just now. I really can't go on pretending to be one person and being another anymore, Boge. It is a living death. I am simply one pretense after another. Only now I recognize it."

Some months before going to France, she told her mentor that she could not read any of the stories she had written without feeling self-contempt. "There is not one," she said, "that I dare show to God." The real reason, and the only reason according to Orage, that Katherine Mansfield went to the Gurdjieff Institute was less dissatisfaction with her craft than dissatisfaction with herself. She went to see if she could heal her secret sorrow of being disunited, and she "worked" on herself with Gurdjieff's guidance, and according to Orage who saw her just a few hours before her death, she died "still radiant in her new attitude."

Her new attitude of seeing life different and then making it different in her new stories was the new literary perspective that she had acquired by becoming more herself at the Institute, an attitude that Hemingway had precociously realized by the time he wrote his first book of stories *In Our Time* that he published before turning twenty-five and which the Macomber and Kilimanjaro stories that he wrote in his mid-thirties were as perfect examples of this attitude as any story could ever be; that's why he said that Mansfield's stories were like near-beer, because he not only knew what real beer tasted like; he had become a connoisseur of real beer.

But despite the fact that Hemingway had Macomber salvage his damaged soul before his wife cut his life short and had Harry die repenting for betraying himself, it still wasn't enough to assuage his conscience and satisfy the longing in his soul to be all that he could be; and after the triumphal elation of his two safari-inspired stories the great writer was forced to go back down into the nitty-gritty of daily life with the despairing knowledge that to ease the aching hollow in his soul he would have to embrace his fate once more and struggle his way back to the top because like the philosopher of the absurd he had to believe that the struggle was enough to make Sisyphus happy;

but it wasn't, despite winning the coveted Nobel Prize for *The Old Man and the Sea*, and that was the tragic self-deception that crushed his tortured soul when shock therapy destroyed his talent and he shot himself to end his suffering.

Hotchner asked Hemingway in his poignant but controversial memoir *Papa Hemingway*, "What do you think happens to a man going on sixty-two when he realizes that he can never write the books and stories he promised himself?"

Hemingway replied, "Look, it doesn't matter that I don't write for a day or a year or ten years as long as the knowledge that I *can* write is solid inside me. But a day without that knowledge, or not being sure of it, is eternity." And Hotchner quotes Hemingway saying (this is after he received shock treatment): "I've got it all and I know what I want it to be but I can't get it down...I can't."

This is why I saw a measure of grace in his suicide, because my high school hero and literary mentor could no longer take up the struggle and had no more reason for living. Suicide was the only graceful way out of his dilemma, and for my money his confessional memoir *A Moveable Feast* was his dying note to the world.

"Ernest lived as long as he could," wrote Arnold Samuelson, the author of the youthful memoir *With Hemingway: A Year in Key West and Cuba*, in a letter to Arnold Gingrich, the publisher of *Esquire*, when he learned of Hemingway's suicide. "His last act was the most deliberate of his life. He had never written about his own suffering. He said it all without words in the language any man can understand," quotes Paul Hendrickson in *Hemingway's Boat*; but the question still remains: why was writing not enough to save Hemingway from himself?

23. The Transcendent Function

As I've come to understand it, the *transcendent function* is an aspect of the natural process of individuation that is engendered by the *enantiodromiac* principle of life that resolves the consciousness of our *being* and *non-being* and we become our true self; and everyone grows in their own identity according to how engaged they are in their *transcendent function*. The more engaged they are, the quicker they grow in their own identity; and the less engaged they are, the slower they grow.

The *enantiodromiac* principle is the principle of *becoming*; the natural process of *being* becoming *non-being*, and *non-being* becoming *being*. As Heraclitus expressed it, nothing stays the same; everything is in a state of flux and forever becoming. "You cannot step into the same river twice," said Jung's inspiration for the process of individuation, which became the central theme of his psychology.

Man is forever becoming. We are always in a state of individuation; from *being* to *non-being*, and from *non-being* to *being*. Or, to be less philosophical, if that is possible, we are forever becoming what we are and what we are not; which is why Sartre came to a dead end with his philosophy of "being and nothingness" in his irresolvable realization, *"I am what I am not, and I am not what I am"* but which I resolved with Gurdjieff's transformative teaching in my realization, *"I am what I am not, and I am not what I am; I am both, but neither: I am Soul."*

We are both our *being* and *non-being*, and our inherent purpose in life is to transcend ourselves and realize our spiritual nature. We are both what we are and what we are not and forever becoming both; and herein lies the mystery of our evolving personality, because we never know where our center of gravity lies. We could be centered in our *being* and be true and authentic and real one moment, and centered in our *non-being* and be false and inauthentic and unreal the next moment; it's all a question of self-awareness.

This is why in Gurdjieff's teaching one has to master the technique of *self-remembering* before he can "work" on himself; and by "work on oneself" Gurdjieff meant transforming the consciousness of what we are not, which he called our false personality. In Jungian terms, our false personality is the repressed *shadow* side of our personality; and transforming the consciousness of our *shadow* self is natural to the process of individuation. So depending upon how engaged we are in our own *transcendent function*, we determine the pace of our own spiritual growth.

Most people are not aware that they are engaged in their own individuation process, but the more conscious one becomes of how life works, the more they participate in the growth of their own identity; and this is neither morally good nor bad. It just is what it is, and we grow in our own *being* and *non-being* according to the values that we live by. This is the natural, but unconscious way of individuation and the way of life for everyone until one is ready to evolve consciously.

There are two kinds of values that we live by. There are positive values that are inherently self-transcending, and there are negative values that are not self-transcending; and by transcending is meant becoming or non-becoming.

Inherently self-transcending values nourish our *being* and transform the consciousness of our *non-being* into *being*; like the noble virtues. Goodness for example, which Socrates deemed to be the most noble of all the virtues, transforms the consciousness of our selfish *shadow* and elevates us to a higher level of *being*. And values that are not self-transcending nourish the consciousness of our *non-being* and transform the consciousness of our *being* into *non-being*; like greed, lust, and avarice which feed our selfish *shadow* self and pull us down to a lower level of *being*. Again, this is neither morally good nor bad; it just is what it is.

This is all very abstruse, but it's all about the natural exchange of energies that goes on in life; a constant give and take that we play out in many different ways in our daily relationships with people, and the more conscious we become of this subtle exchange of energies the more we master the game of life.

Gurdjieff was a master of the game of life; so much so that he could put on any guise he wanted to suit whatever purpose he intended. This is why no one has ever been able to pin Gurdjieff down. But the central theme of Gurdjieff's teaching was to learn how to use life to grow in *being* and "create" our own soul.

Hemingway was also a master of the game of life; which is why he was so successful in everything that engaged his interest, like deep sea fishing. But the difference between Gurdjieff and Hemingway was that Gurdjieff played the game of life with conscious intent and Hemingway was blind to life's inherent purpose.

Gurdjieff became a master of his own individuation (which is what he meant by taking evolution into our own hands), and Hemingway became a slave to his own individuation; which is why his selfish *shadow* pulled him down into deeper and deeper depths of depression, and out of despair he killed himself.

This is why I fell in love with C. G. Jung, because like my high school hero he also had a great desire to succeed in life; but unlike Hemingway, upon achieving "honor, power, wealth, knowledge, and every human happiness" Jung's desire for these trappings ceased, and horror came over him because of what it had cost him to achieve his success. "My soul, where are you?" he asked; and he went on a quest for the soul he had neglected to achieve the trappings of his great success.

Hemingway never had such a *metanoic* change of heart, which is why he kept repeating his narcissistic pleasure-seeking life (marrying four times and falling in love with ridiculously young women as he vainly tried to recapture his youth; but it gave him great material for writing); and in the end the oppressive burden of his immortalizing literary fame and undisciplined self-indulgence so soured his life that it drove him to commit suicide, whereas Jung selflessly served his fellow man right to the end of his octogenarian sweet life, and despite their separate paths I admire them both for the courage, integrity, and genius of their individual lives.

I know the path that Jung took to realize wholeness and singleness of self, which he confirmed for me as I read *The Red Book*, and I also know the path that Hemingway took because I had to master the way of *non-being* that destroyed my literary mentor's life; this is why these two men were brought together to set the record straight on my own self-becoming. And I have to thank the movie *Hemingway and Gellhorn* for pulling me back to Hemingway, because this opened me up the *enantiodromiac* principle of life that is the soul of all great literature.

The saddest truth that I had to accept as I worked my way through the darkness of my own *non-being* in my search for my true self, was that *we are not meant to know the meaning and purpose of life*; and the moment one finds out, they are derided. This is why Socrates gave us a heads up when he told us about the prisoners in the cave that escaped into the light and then went back down into the cave to free their fellow prisoners and were mocked and ridiculed for their fabulous tales of real life outside the cave of shadows and reflections; so, what's a writer to do?

Gurdjieff taught me well in his advice to take a vow of silence, because he knew from his own experience that there is only self-initiation into the mysteries of life; but a writer is a writer and is driven to tell the truth, which is why the deepest truths of life have always been written in myth and allegory that touch the soul of man but preoccupy the mind forever, but where does that leave literature?

This was my dilemma, which I had no way of resolving; that's why I had to rely upon my own *transcendent function*. I had no thought of writing my novel *What Would I Say Today If I Were to Die Tomorrow?* That idea for my first novel came to me in a synoptic flash of creative insight that gripped my soul and compelled me to get it out in the same short eight week period of time that it took my high school hero to write his first novel *The Sun Also Rises*; and this set me up for the next stage of my journey through life to relocate to Georgian Bay where I had seven past-life regressions which I worked into my novel *Cathedral of My Past Lives*.

But I had such an explosion of consciousness with my regressions and writing *Cathedral of My Past Lives* that it set free my "Soul talk" books, which I dictated into my mini recorder as I commuted to and from my work each day, the first book being *The Way of Soul* that pulled Carl Jung into my dream life; and my "Soul talk" books inspired my novel *The Waking Dream* in which Jung played a central role.

But no sooner did I complete *The Waking Dream* and I was compelled by my Muse to write *Jesus Wears Dockers*, because I could not resist the urge to decode the sayings of Jesus in the style of modern literature; and upon completion of *Jesus Wears Dockers* I was gripped again to write the sequel *St. Paul's Conceit* to further decode Jesus Christ's teaching of spiritual liberation from the prison of the *enantiodromiac* principle of life. And this prepared me for my novel *My Unborn Child*, in which I pitted the contentious issue of abortion with the liberating perspective of reincarnation in a dialectic of creative resolution; but the poor reception of my bold experiment told me just how difficult it was to expand the parameters of modern literature— the direct, but ironic opposite of what happened to my hero Hemingway with his literary experiment *Green Hills of Africa* which failed to engage the creative dialectic of his *transcendent function* and fell flat.

We're not meant to know the meaning and purpose of life; this is why it takes so long for literature to break through the impenetrable walls of the status quo. But the irony is that society has outgrown the existential paradigm of literature what with reputable physicists like Amit Goswami writing about *Consciousness* being the ground of all being (*The Self-aware*

Universe), and respectable neurosurgeons like Dr. Eben Alexander writing about irrefutable out-of-body experiences (*Proof of Heaven*), and mainstream psychiatrists like Dr. Brian L. Weiss writing about reincarnation as a principle of soul's evolution through life (*Many Lives, Many Masters*); literature has to catch up to the evolving spiritual consciousness of society, and it's the writer's artistic responsibility to help make it so.

This is why I was called to write my novel *Tea with Grace, A Story of Synchronicity and Platonic Love,* so I could affect my reader with the dialectic of creative writing and break through the inflexible Christian paradigm of the single life and heaven and hell; and this is why I was compelled to watch *Hemingway and Gellhorn,* because my inner guidance knew what I had to do to help expand the stifling existential paradigm of modern literature and awaken the reader to the *enantiodromiac* principle of life and *transcendent function.*

24. My Gift from Ernest Hemingway

I have so much love, respect, and admiration for Gurdjieff that I would love nothing more than to go to his grave in Fontainebleau-Avon, France and place a single yellow rose on his gravestone, and as much as I would love to place him in my pantheon of heroes with Hemingway and Jung, this remarkable man stands alone in a class all by himself; and I honestly don't know what to call him.

Without Gurdjieff's teaching I have no idea if I would have solved the mystery of my *shadow* self, which I was driven to do; and I could have ended up a very sad and disillusioned man—which, if what I was told by Ascended Master St. Padre Pio who was the inspiration for my novel *Healing with Padre Pio*, I did; because he told me that I came back to live my same life over again "to achieve a different outcome."

But this is not the place to talk about parallel lives, despite the fact that this concept is being explored by quantum physicists and writers like Kate Atkinson with ground-breaking novels like *Life after Life;* so I will stick to my current life in which Gurdjieff helped me achieve the outcome of finding my true self; and for this I owe him such an enormous debt of gratitude that the only way I can ever repay him would be to pass on the secret of his teaching; and herein lies my dilemma.

Gurdjieff was wrong. He believed that not everyone is born with an immortal soul; only certain people who manage through extraordinary life circumstances to crystalize the vital life force and create an embryonic soul, circumstances that Gurdjieff created with his remarkable teaching. But so difficult was it to succeed with his teaching that in all the books that I read on Gurdjieff and his students, I never came across one person who spoke of "creating" their own soul. Which was why so many of Gurdjieff's students became disillusioned and left the

Work. But despite the misperception of his premise, his teaching worked all the same to quicken the individuation of the self; and for this I will always be grateful because it helped me find my true self.

I can't remember when, but a year or so after I experienced my immortal self in my mother's kitchen that memorable day while she was kneading bread dough on the kitchen table, I dreamt of one of my favorite students of Gurdjieff's teaching, Dr. Maurice Nicoll, who was a student of C. G. Jung before going to the Gurdjieff Institute in Fontainebleau-Avon to study the Work for a year and who went back to London, England to set up his medical practice on Harley Street and study the Work with P. D. Ouspensky and write about it in his *Commentaries*; but in my dream he had left the Work and was studying a new path, which happened to be the same spiritual path that I had taken up after leaving Gurdjieff's teaching too.

Dr. Nicoll died in 1953, but the new path that he was living "over there" was not introduced to our modern world until a decade later, in the early 1960s, which was another confirmation that our life continues on the other side when we shuffle off this mortal coil; and despite the fact that I had embraced my new path because it was right for me, I had an overwhelming nostalgic need to reconnect with Gurdjieff and his teaching; which was why Dr. Nicoll came to me in my dream.

I thanked him for all the guidance he had given me with his psychological commentaries on the Work and for other books that he had written, my favorite being his interpretation of some of Christ's parables called *The New Man*, and then we talked about our new path that we had both embraced; and he told me how the Work had prepared him for our new path as it had prepared me, and I woke up from my dream with him shouting in my ear so I would remember my dream, *"The Work is Spirit! The Work is Spirit! The Work is Spirit!"*

This was Dr. Nicoll's way of confirming that the omniscient guiding force of life is the essential principle of all spiritual paths and teachings, which we had talked about in my dream; and after my dream I no longer had that nostalgic need to reconnect with Gurdjieff's teaching because I had outgrown it and was right to embrace a higher aspect of the secret teaching in our new path. And then a short while later I had another dream of meeting a very devout student of Gurdjieff's teaching who became offended when I suggested that she would one day also outgrow the Work and would have to move on to another path—

"No way!" she interrupted. *"I'll never leave the Work! It's my life!"*

I didn't expected such a strong reaction, and I tried to calm her down. "Of course the Work is your life; I understand that. All I'm saying is that the Work is only one aspect of the secret teachings of the Way. There are others. And when you're ready, you'll be introduced to another aspect of the secret teaching, and another, and quite possibly another until you and the Way become one..."

It took a while, but I managed to calm her down; and we parted on friendly terms. But when I woke up from my dream of this beautiful thirty-five year old passionate student of Gurdjieff's teaching in a city on the other side not unlike any modern city over here in North America, I reflected on her commitment and smiled to myself because that's exactly how I felt when I was caught up in my own passion for the Work; and after thirty-five years of living my new spiritual path after dropping Gurdjieff's teaching, I was finally ready to embrace my own personal path of creative writing that my return to Hemingway had awakened me to; that's why my inner guidance insisted that I watch the movie *Hemingway and Gellhorn*, true to the old saying, "When the student is ready, the teacher appears."

If I had made this story up, I would never believe it; but because it's my life I know the facts and I have to smile at how choreographed my life has been, because I've come full circle right back to my high school hero.

I had to run the race just to get to the starting line where both Hemingway and Jung and every person born into their own destiny are meant to be; but why was I so far behind myself that it took most of my life just to catch up to where my two heroes began by taking their own destined path through life—Hemingway through writing, and Jung through psychiatry? And was this the reason for my envy of the gifted writer who introduced me to literature?

As much as I loved reading Hemingway in high school and for many years after, I resented his gift for making writing seem so damn easy; and there were times when I became so disgusted with myself that I refused to even read him, and his posthumous books sat on my shelf for years—except for *A Moveable Feast*, which moved me to tears and confirmed my admiration for his amazing gift.

But even so, I still could not bring myself to finish reading him; and in a strange kind of way, it was like Hemingway reserving his Joseph Conrad, who was one of his writer heroes, because he wanted to save him for when he really needed Conrad to give him the boost he needed to buoy up his flagging spirit.

Had I not found my true self, I would never have figured it out; but because I resolved the issue of my own *shadow*, I came to see that we have two destinies in life: one karmic, and personal; and the other spiritual, and impersonal; and our purpose in life is to reconcile our two destinies into one path, which becomes our own individual way through life. And then like Frank Sinatra we can say, "I did it my way." This is why some people are born into their own destiny and others like me have to catch up to themselves before they can live their own life.

From one life to the next, we create our own karma and grow and evolve in our own individual talents that determines our karmic destiny, all the while pulled by the teleological imperative of our encoded spiritual destiny—which is to realize wholeness and singleness of self. Just as an acorn seed HAS to become an oak tree and not a donkey, so are we spiritually destined to become who we are meant to be; but the irony of our spiritual destiny is that it is shaped by our karmic destiny, and herein lies the impenetrable mystery of our own individuality.

The medieval Persian poet Rumi, whose poetry Coleman Barks has made accessible and immensely popular with his endearing translations, spoke to this mystery: "These leaves, our bodily personalities, seem identical, /but the globe of soul fruit /we make, /each is elaborately /unique." Rumi confirms what I discovered in my quest for my true self, that we all have an outer self in our personality, which he calls "leaves" that seem the same in every person; and we all have an inner self, which he called a "globe of soul fruit," which is unique to every person.

Above and beyond our genetic makeup, which predetermines our biology and to a large extent our psychic make-up, because we have free will we create our own karmic destiny; and our karmic destiny determines the uniqueness of our "globe of soul fruit," because no two people have the same karmic relationship with life. So despite how similar our "bodily personalities" may appear to be, our "globe of soul fruit" is determined by the karma that we create and is "elaborately unique," and from life to life we grow in our spiritual nature through the process of karmic individuation until we are ready to bear the "globe of soul fruit" of our spiritual destiny. When we come to this point in our evolution where we are ready to bear the fruit of our individuation, our karmic destiny is brought into alignment with our spiritual destiny and we live our life in the singular purpose of becoming the unique person that we are meant to be, like Ernest Hemingway and C. G. Jung.

Hemingway was destined to become a great writer, and Jung was destined to "kindle a light in the darkness of mere being," but I had to work my whole life to bring my karmic destiny into alignment with my spiritual destiny so that I could forge a path to call my own; and my return to Hemingway has brought me full circle, and now I can join the race and be my own person. *God, it's taken me a long time to find my own writer's voice!*

25. Making the Connection

In addition to the implicit 10,000-Hour Rule that has become fixed in social consciousness thanks to *New Yorker* writer Malcolm Gladwell's book *Outliers*, the blossoming of our individual talent presupposes much more than the eye can see; and as difficult as it may be to acknowledge in the pages of the *New Yorker*, we have to live many lifetimes to evolve in the consciousness of our own individual genius—like my heroes Hemingway and Jung; and we can't realize the fruit of our inherent genius unless we make the connection with our inner self, which makes the crucial difference between those who succeed in life and those that don't.

There are many people in the world that have the natural talent of their own individuated karmic genius that has taken many lifetimes to evolve, but unless they connect with their inner self they will never bear the fruit of their individual genius; which gives credence to the 10,000-Hour Rule that facilitates this connection.

"Even Mozart—the greatest musical prodigy of all time—couldn't hit his stride until he had his ten thousand hours in. Practice isn't the thing you do once you're good. It's the thing you do that makes you good," says Gladwell in *Outliers*; and he goes on to illustrate his enlightening principle of the 10,000-Hour Rule with the incredible stories of how the Beetles and the founder of Microsoft Bill Gates became so amazingly successful—and all because they took advantage of the opportunities that allowed them to realize the fruit of their inherent genius.

"All the outliers we've looked at so far were the beneficiaries of some kind of unusual opportunity. Lucky breaks don't seem like the exception with software billionaires and rock bands and star athletes. They seem like the rule," says Gladwell, as he explores the logic that makes people successful; and after all the books that I have read on Ernest Hemingway and Carl Jung I can vouch that they too were fortuitously blessed with synchronistic opportunities that helped launch their careers and realize the potential of their inherent genius.

I use the phrase *synchronistic opportunities* on purpose, because the mysterious principle of synchronicity seems to come into play in our life whenever we're in need of special guidance on our journey through life (which I've personally experienced at critical junctures in my life, like my "lucky" discovery of Gurdjieff's teaching); and when one has evolved to the point where they are ready to realize the fruit of their karmic evolution, synchronicity presents them with opportunities to help them complete their journey to their true self. And there are countless stories of how synchronicity has opened the door for successful people, as Robert H. Hopcke tells us in *There Are No Accidents, Synchronicity and the Stories of Our Lives.*

Carl Jung coined the word *synchronicity*, which he defined as an a-causal connecting principle but which I've come to recognize as the loving principle of the omniscient guiding force of life; and as dismissively esoteric as this may sound, Jung offered us a credibly exoteric explanation within the paradigm of psychology: "The synchronistic principle possesses properties that may help to clear up the body-soul problem. Above all it is the fact of causeless order, or rather, of meaningful orderliness that may throw light on psychophysical parallelism. The 'absolute knowledge' which is characteristic of synchronistic phenomena, a knowledge not mediated by the sense organs, supports the hypothesis of a self-subsistent meaning, or even expresses its existence. *Such a form of existence can only be transcendental*, since, as the knowledge of future or spatially distant events shows, it is contained in a psychically relative space and time, that is to say in an irrepresentable space-time continuum" (*Synchronicity*, C. G. Jung, Italics mine, p.90).

The "body-soul problem," speaks to our two destinies— our karmic destiny, which we create by the choices we make;

and our spiritual destiny, which is pre-determined and teleologically driven. In effect, we create our karmic destiny by the choices we make, and if the merciful principle of synchronicity presents us with opportunities to realize our inherent karmic potential, then we can't point our finger to the heavens and shout like Gloucester in Shakespeare's tragic play *King Lear*, "As flies to wonton boys are we to the gods. They kill us for their sport!"

God has nothing to do with our success, or lack of it; it's all a question of the choices we make, like the young Hemingway taking advantage of the synchronistic opportunity presented to him to write for the *Kansas City Star* which proved to be invaluable training for his career, and the synchronistic opportunity that opened the door for him to write for the *Toronto Star* and *Star Weekly*, which in turn gave him an opportunity to go to Paris to write as a foreign correspondent, the city where Hemingway racked up the hours for his apprenticeship, which added up to more than the allotted ten thousand to launch his fledgling career with his first novel *The Sun Also Rises*; just as Carl Jung exceeded ten thousand hours of practice and study at the Bergholzli psychiatric hospital in Zurich which prepared him to take advantage of the opportunity to study with Sigmund Freud who in turn created the opportunity for Jung to break away from Freud's reductionist school of thought and launch his own successful career with his groundbreaking theory of the unconscious.

Contrary to what Macbeth tells us, life is not a tale told by an idiot full of sound and fury signifying nothing; life is meaningful and merciful if we make choices that don't lead us to dead ends that so restrict our perspective we can't see beyond our own coveted needs, as Ernest Hemingway began to do when fame clouded his judgment and boxed him into a corner with no way out but suicide.

That was the tragedy of my high school hero's life. He made some courageous life-changing decisions in his youth that nurtured his writing career, like joining the American Red Cross and going to Italy where he got wounded by an Austrian mortar shell on the Italian front which led to his first real love experience with nurse Agnes von Kurowsky that gave him the material he needed for his famous novel *A Farewell to Arms* which he wrote after he clocked up the hours for his apprenticeship in Paris where he connected with his inner self with such *daemonic* passion that he realized the fruit of his inherent genius at an early age with his first book of stories *In Our Time;* but the connection with his inner self began to be seriously inhibited by the betrayal of his love for Hadley, the only woman in his brilliant career who loved him the way he needed to be loved to complete his life, whereas the choice that my other hero C. G. Jung made to reclaim his lost soul when he realized that he had blindly forfeited it for his worldly success opened the door to the spiritually claustrophobic room that he had boxed himself into (which he illustrated with a painting of his own *shadow* self in *The Red Book*) and he went in search of his lost soul and kindled a light so bright in the darkness of mere being that it will take society many years to appreciate his invaluable contribution to the world.

The poet Archibald MacLeish, who was a close friend of Ernest Hemingway before the great writer turned on him as he turned on most of his friends throughout his life (and in vicious, nasty ways as he courageously and/or foolishly reveals in his memoir *A Moveable Feast* and private letters), wrote a poem that caught the essence of my literary mentor's tragic life. Quoting from *Hemingway's Boat*, MacLeish says: "'Veteran out of the war before he was twenty: /Famous at twenty-five: /Thirty a master—' but also saying in a line immediately above: 'And what became of Hemingway? Fame became of him,'" implying with poetic genius how fame destroyed Ernest Hemingway's life.

"Did Hemingway want a 'wholly different kind of association—one he could dominate as a matter of course?' Those are Archibald MacLeish's words, in a letter four years after Hemingway's suicide," writes Paul Hendrickson. "What is arguable is that so many of Hemingway's deepest relationships, especially literary friendships, going back to Paris, and even before Paris, would never be the same after the 1930s," after his fame had been secured with *A Farewell to Arms*. "One by one, he'd lose them all—well, if not lose, exactly, estrange them all, in lesser and greater ways." But Hemingway was such a paradoxical human being that the betrayed but candid poet Archibald MacLeish also said: "It would be so abundantly easy to describe Ernest in terms, all of which would be historically correct, which would present him as a completely insufferable human being. Actually, he was one of the most profoundly human and spiritually powerful creatures that I have ever known." That's the same conclusion that Hendrickson came to in his wonderfully researched and fair-minded portrayal of my high school hero's life in *Hemingway's Boat*; he believed that Hemingway "was on a lifelong quest for sainthood, and not just literary sainthood, and that at nearly every turn, he defeated himself, and in what he believed in" (*Hemingway's Boat*, pp. 156, 158 respectively).

And how did this happen? Hendrickson quotes the dying writer Harry from "The Snows of Kilimanjaro," which Hemingway confessed to be his most autobiographical story: "By betrayals of himself, and what he believed in."

As Harry's life fell apart by his self-betrayals, so Hendrickson feels that Hemingway's life fell apart because of "the seductions of celebrity and the sin of pridefulness and the curse of megalomania and the wastings of booze and, not least, the onslaughts of bipolarism," and I don't disagree; but that's precisely what made Hemingway the great writer that he became just as I intuited from the movie *Hemingway and Gellhorn* which forced me to erupt in a volcanic burst of emotional awareness, *"He had to be a prick to become the great writer that he became!"*

Had Hemingway not reflected both sides of his personality—his dark *shadow* side and his conscious ego-personality which he created with such passion for life-experience that he exhausted everyone who knew him—his *enantiodromiac* process of self-becoming would not have added the "tremulous" depth of character and complexity to his writing; but he was such a miserable bastard as well as one of the most sensitive writers in the world—supported by *Life* magazine's article "The Last Words Hemingway Wrote" in its August 21, 1963 issue, a letter to nine year old Fritz, the dying son of Hemingway's friend Dr. Saviers— that his work will continue to be read by generations to come.

When Paul Hendrickson went to Ketchum and talked with Pierre Saviers, a practicing psychotherapist, about Hemingway's letter to Pierre's brother Fritz that is framed and hung in a hallway at Sun Valley Lodge, Pierre responded thoughtfully, though somewhat morosely, "Hemingway? He knew he was done. And he knows Fritz is done. But he still wants to save him, even as he wants to save himself. You know about the damsel in distress tied to the railroad track? Well, that's us. You recognize yourself there, and you want to save yourself. It's all layered. The way I see all this is that part of what we do in this life is conscious. And the rest of it is unconscious. Maybe this is the best we can ever say" (*Hemingway's Boat*, p. 465).

Perhaps; but it's the writer's job to get to the bottom of things, which is what made Hemingway such a great writer of the human condition—despite the fact that he became so disconnected from his inner self that he could not overcome the hold that the destructive *shadow* side of his personality had over him. Hemingway fought the battle, but whether he won or lost is a matter of personal perspective.

26. The Individuation Process

Central to Carl Jung's psychology, which he called Analytical Psychology to distinguish it from Freudian psychoanalysis that he had to break away from because Freud could not embrace Jung's unfolding perspective on the psyche, is what Jung came to call the "individuation process," which could also be called "coming to selfhood," or "self-realization" and which I simply refer to as self-becoming.

In her succinct and elegant biography *Carl Jung, Wounded Healer of the Soul*, Irish-born Australian author and broadcaster Claire Dunne elucidates the central theme of Jung's ground-breaking psychology: "Individuation is the experience of a natural law, an inner self-regulating process by which man becomes a whole human being acknowledging and living the total range of himself. In the process the ego is ultimately faced with something larger than itself, a force that it yields to and serves. The human being thus recognizes itself as both material and spiritual, conscious and unconscious." And she furnishes her elucidation with an enhanced definition from one of Jung's private letters: "Individuation does not only mean that man has become truly human as distinct from animal, but that he is to become partially divine as well. That means practically that he becomes adult, responsible for his existence knowing that he does not only depend on God, but that God depends on him" (*Carl Jung, Wounded Healer of the Soul*, pp.83-85).

Man is both human and divine, which I can confirm with one of my past-life regressions where I was brought back to the Body of God and experienced myself as an immortal atom of God (which I came to recognize as a soul seed, or what the poet John Keats called an "atom of perception" that has not yet "acquired' its own identity), and in the same regression I was brought back to my first primordial human lifetime as the alpha male of a group of higher primates where I experienced the dawning of the "I" of my own identity that set me apart from the rest of my group that had not yet constelled enough consciousness of life to give birth to their own reflective self, however rudimentary; this is why I can expand upon the boundaries of Jung's individuation process that he was forced by the imperative of his empirical science to limit to one lifetime alone, because I was also regressed to some of my other past lives which allowed me to see how the natural process of individuation is governed by the spiritual laws of karma and reincarnation.

So as much as I would love to keep my understanding of how life works within the existential paradigm of one lifetime alone, which defines the human condition that Hemingway reflected in his work with artistic genius, I have no choice but to "tell it the way it was" in my experience of the individuation process which I took into my own hands with Gurdjieff's teaching; and the biggest lesson that I learned on the journey to my true self was that we *have* to grow into the person we are meant to be just as the acorn seed *has* to grow into an oak tree. And herein lies the dilemma that drove my high school hero and literary mentor to suicide, because he could not bring himself to take responsibility for his own individuation and let the unresolved *shadow* side of his personality rule his conflicted egotistical life.

But why? Why would the man who read two of the most inspiring books that address the individuation process—*Dark Night of the Soul,* by St. John of the Cross, and *The Imitation of Christ,* by Thomas Kempis—while writing the novel whose basic theme was man's struggle with himself, *The Old Man and the Sea*; why would Hemingway not comply with his artistic conscience that his hero Santiago had awakened him to not work his way out of his own dark night of the soul as my other hero Carl Jung chose to do when the natural individuation process of his life brought him as far as it could take him? Why could not Hemingway take responsibility for his life as Jung did and work on the *shadow* side of his personality and save himself?

Given Santiago's triumphant struggle to save his marlin from the sharks, why did my high school hero refuse to take on the battle with the "sharks" of his own dark *shadow* side; or was it enough for him to redeem himself through his writing alone? Was that how he appeased his conscience?

From everything that I've read since my return to Hemingway (half a dozen new biographies and most of his stories), I have to conclude that Hemingway's life reflected what the Stoic philosopher captured in his poem; and at the risk of repetition, it's worth quoting Cleanthes again because my high school hero made himself a slave to his own spiritual imperative because he wanted the best of all possible worlds, and like Sisyphus proudly defied the god of destiny:

Lead me Zeus,
And thou, o destiny
The way I am bid by thee to go.
To follow I am willing,
For were I recusant,
I do but make myself a slave,
And still must follow.

For all of his creative genius, I was forced to see that my high school hero was like a spoiled and petulant child who refused to take responsibility for the selfish choices he made throughout his life that so inhibited his self-becoming that even the redemptive power of his writing could not save him from himself, and he made himself a slave to the spiritual imperative of his life.

That's why his good friend Archibald MacLeish who took him in when he left Hadley while waiting to get together with Pauline but whom Hemingway later betrayed said, "he was one of the most profoundly human and spiritually powerful creatures that I have ever known," and why the author of *Hemingway's Boat* felt that he was on a "lifelong quest for sainthood, and not just literary sainthood, and that at nearly every turn, he defeated himself, and what he believed in."

The writer with the power to redeem himself in his stories and the insufferable bastard that he became were one and the same creature, which I finally came to realize as I watched the movie *Hemingway and Gellhorn*; and to separate the two does not do the man justice, because he simply would not have become the great writer that he became had he worked his way out of his *enantiodromiac* dilemma.

He had to be a sensitive bastard, or *monstre sacré* as the French like to say, to write the way he did; and I have to credit the British actor Clive Owen who faithfully captured the essence of Hemingway's character and the Australian actress Nicole Kidman who faithfully captured the defiant soul of Hemingway's third wife for magnifying the truth of their tempestuous relationship with such artistic brilliance that it awakened me to the *enantiodromiac* principle of life that launched me back to Hemingway and set me firmly on the path of my writer self, which I know from years of writing just how demanding it can be.

"Writing is something that you can never do as well as it can be done," said the Nobel laureate in a letter to Ivan Kashkin. "It is a perpetual challenge and it is more difficult than anything else that I have ever done—so I do it. And it makes me happy when I do it well" (*Ernest Hemingway, Selected Letters, 1917-1961*, p. 419); and the lesson that I can take away from my return to Hemingway is just how much courage it takes to write about one's fucked-up life—if one may be allowed to use this most appropriate expletive, which I know Hemingway would employ but then delete for his publisher's sake, and propriety.

27. That's the Way It Was For Me

I didn't expect to be pulled into the deep end of the pool with this memoir, but I've never had a choice when it comes to writing; I have to go where my creative unconscious takes me, and now it's pulling me into the deepest part of the pool with an experience that I had almost forty years ago but which I never understood until I connected the dots with my past-life regressions and made sense of my experience of going back through time to when there was no life on Planet Earth.

As I have come to believe (actually, this was forced upon me; otherwise I would never have embraced it), we are not meant to know the meaning and purpose of life; but I went so far out of my way to find my true self that the meaning and purpose of life revealed itself to me, starting with my experience of going back through time to when life began on Planet Earth.

I was living at my parents' home and was into my second or third year of my house-painting business, all the while living Gurdjieff's teaching; and one spring day I had the afternoon off and took out a chair and sat in the back yard of our home to sit and ponder and take in the warm rays of the spring sun.

It had been a long cold winter, as most winters in Northwestern Ontario are, and it felt good to be sitting outside in the warm spring sun; and I leaned my chair back and rested my head on the warm stucco wall of our family home, and I closed my eyes and let the sun warm my face and soothe my soul.

Soon I felt myself drifting, floating back through time. I didn't stop to think about what was happening, I just went with it; and before I knew it I was being pulled back through the weeks, the months, the years, the decades, the centuries, the millennia, the eons, further, and further, and further back; and I saw Planet Earth from a distance, not unlike how Carl Jung saw the Earth when he had his out-of-body experience after his heart attack which he recounts in his memoir *Memories, Dreams, Reflections*; but only in my experience the Earth was not a beautiful shining blue globe, it was dull and grey and barren of all life—absolutely barren, because life had not yet begun on Planet Earth.

And I observed the world not thinking about what I was doing; I was just an impersonal witness to the experience, as though I was outside my thinking mind. And then I saw the vaporous gases of the planet rise up and mingle with the vaporous gases in the sky, and then I experienced something that scientists would sell their mother to experience—the genesis of life on Planet Earth.

As the gases from the Earth blended with the gases from the sky, they formed amino acids, which scientists have shown to be the first building blocks of life; and as the amino acids formed, I experienced myself entering into them like I was being poured into an empty vessel. And the moment I became one with the amino acids, I experienced the genesis of life on Planet Earth.

As miraculous as this was, I did not experience it as a miracle; I just experienced the inception of life on Earth—the exact moment when life began on our planet. And once I had this experience I felt myself being pulled forward through time, through the eons, millennia, centuries—further, and further, and further all the way back to the present moment of my life sitting in my chair soaking in the warm rays of the sun, and I opened my eyes and sat and stared in stark wonder.

I had no idea what had just happened; all I knew was that it happened, and I did not know what to make of it. And I would not know what it meant for many years, not until I resolved the dilemma of my *enantiodromiac* life and gave birth to my spiritual self in my mother's kitchen that day while she was kneading bread dough on the kitchen table and years later after I had my seven past-life regressions, only then did I connect the dots and make sense of my experience.

Because I had resolved the paradox of my self-becoming by "working" on myself with Gurdjieff's teaching (as well as my *Royal Dictum*, my personal ethic, the sayings of Jesus, and long distance running), I knew that I was Soul, the resolved self-consciousness of my *being* and *non-being*; so when I was brought back to the Body of God in my regression and experienced myself as an atom of God that had not yet acquired its own identity, I realized that I had experienced myself as an atom of divine perception without self-realization.

I was a soul without a self; and then I went back to my first human life where I experienced the dawning of my reflective self-consciousness, and from incarnation to incarnation I grew in the consciousness of my reflective self through the natural process of individuation until the *enantiodromiac* principle of life could take me no further and I had to take evolution into my own hands to realize the wholeness and singleness of self of my spiritual destiny, which I did with Gurdjieff's teaching. So the dawning of my reflective self in my first human life, and the birth of my spiritual self in my current lifetime, and my regression to the Body of God all added up to the meaning and purpose of life—which was to grow and evolve through life to expand the Consciousness of God; which was the same conclusion that Jung came to when he said that God depends upon man as much as man depends on God.

So when I went back through time and experienced the genesis of life on Planet Earth—which was years before I gave birth to my spiritual self and many years before my past-life regressions—I had no idea how I could be responsible for kick-starting the life process on Earth; but once I realized that I was Soul, which I knew from my experience of having resolved the *enantiodromiac* process of my life and experiencing myself as Soul, I knew that Soul was responsible for the inception of life on Earth; and because Soul was the divine consciousness of my spiritual self, it was only logical to conclude that Soul initiated the *enantiodromiac* principle of becoming and was the ground of all *being* and *non-being*. This is why when I gave birth to my spiritual self I had the realization: *I am want I am not, and I am not what I am; I am both, but neither: I am Soul.* In short, Soul is who we are, the *I Am* Consciousness of life; but we have to evolve through life to resolve the paradoxical nature of our individual *enantiodromiac* process until we give birth to our spiritual self; only then will we know that the meaning and purpose of life is to expand the Consciousness of God by becoming our true self. This is why when Moses asked the voice on Mount Sinai to identify itself, God replied: *"I Am that I Am."* Meaning, God is God becoming God. That's why God gave Moses the Ten Commandments to help man take evolution into his own hands and realize his divine nature.

And this is why I've always been fascinated by Hemingway. Something about his life intrigued me; and it wasn't until the movie *Hemingway and Gellhorn* awakened me to the *enantiodromiac* process of Hemingway's life did I begin to make sense of his paradoxical nature. But I have to thank C. G. Jung for helping me connect the dots; and, of course, Gurdjieff whose teaching helped me take evolution into my own hands so I could resolve the paradox of my own life and find my true self. And as incredible as this may be, that's the way it was for me.

28. The Healing Power of Writing

"The time to work is shorter all the time and if you waste it you feel you have committed a sin for which there is no forgiveness," said my literary mentor; and then added, "Writing is a hard business, but nothing makes you feel better."

Why did Hemingway feel better when he was writing? What is it about writing—specifically writing stories—that made him feel better? Did it, for example, make him feel better to play out his anger at his father in his story "Fathers and Sons" by having Nickolas Adams imagine blowing his father to hell?

When Greg Bellow was asked what kind of relationship he had with his famous Nobel Laureate father Saul Bellow, he replied, "Read his novels. It's all there." And so is Hemingway's life all there, in his stories and novels; was that why he wrote, to get all the undealt-with emotions out of his system? In "Fathers and Sons" he did have his alter ego Nicolas Adams say, "If he wrote he could get rid of it. He had gotten rid of many things by writing them."

There's a healing power to writing, and writers write to work their way through troubling states of mind; that's why Hemingway refused to see a "head doctor" when "black-ass" depression and delusions of persecution began to seriously affect his mind after he won the Nobel Prize for Literature, because writing always made him feel better; but when his memory (which he called his "greatest asset" and his wife Mary called a "tape recorder in his head") was damaged by the electroshock therapy that he received at the Mayo Clinic where his wife and Ketchum Idaho friend Dr. Saviers had him taken under the cover of getting him treatment for high blood pressure, my high school hero could no longer tap into the healing power of writing and he lost his reason for living; that's why he committed suicide.

When Joan Didion's husband the writer and literary critic John Gregory Dunne died suddenly of a heart attack, she was so grief-stricken that she had to write to save herself; and she wrote *The Year of Magical Thinking*, which won the 2005 National Book Award for Nonfiction; and Miriam Toews, the Canadian author of *A Complicated Kindness*, wrote her most autobiographical novel *All My Puny Sorrows* to work through the grief of her depressed sister's suicide, just as Francisco Goldman wrote through the unbearable sorrow of his young wife's tragic death in *Say Her Name*; so there's no doubt of the healing power of writing.

Hemingway has given me a new love for literature, because in my return to my high school hero and literary mentor I've sounded the deepest depths of the creative process, and I've been emboldened to write the stories that I've always lacked the courage to write—like my sexual experience that catapulted me into my quest for my true self, and my experience with a Christian solar cult teaching that did irreparable damage to my eyesight. Actually I started that story which I called "The Sunworshipper," but I could never bring myself to finish it; but thanks to Hemingway I can write these stories now, and a few others that I dared not tackle.

When Hemingway showed his story "Up in Michigan" to his mentor Gertrude Stein, she told him that it was *inaccrrochable*; a French world, by which the patron of the arts meant that is was like a painting that could not be hung in public because of its sexual content; but it got published despite her condescending opinion.

Hemingway's writing credo was to tell it the way it was, and whether the rape/seduction scene in the story was inspired by his own experience or not doesn't really matter (I suspect it probably was), because he wanted his writing to be as true to life as it could be, and if he got lucky it would be even more true than life.

"All good books are alike in that they are truer than if they had really happened," he wrote in *Esquire*, December 1934

("Old Newsman Writes: A Letter from Cuba"); and it was this quality of being truer than life that compelled him to write short stories and novels, because this was his moral compass that kept him honest—like the description of his youngest son Gigi in his posthumous novel *Islands in the Stream*: "He was a boy born to be quite wicked who was being very good and he carried his wickedness around him transformed into a sort of teasing gaiety. But he was a bad boy and the others knew it and he knew it. He was just being good while his badness grew inside him."

The "wickedness" that Hemingway saw in his son Gigi was a reflection of the repressed dark *shadow* side of his own personality, and the author of *Hemingway's Boat* Paul Hendrickson goes so far as to say that he feels Hemingway's third son Gigi, who loved to dress in woman's clothes from a very early age, played out in real life his father's hidden ("wicked") androgynous sexuality; which doesn't really surprise me, because children inherent their *family shadow*.

But even if the sins of the parents are visited upon the children, as I believe they are through the medium of the *family shadow*, it doesn't absolve us of the responsibility of our self-becoming; because to become the person we are meant to be we have to take evolution into our own hands, and we can't blame our parents for our own life, which I did for many years before I saw the light.

Once I grasped how the natural individuation process of life worked, which after my return to Hemingway I learned was driven by the *enantiodromiac* principle of life, I realized that the only person who can save us from ourselves is ourselves because karma is a personal responsibility; and this includes the karma that we inherent from our parents through the medium of our *family shadow*.

That's why Hemingway loved to write fiction; because the liberating power of his *transcendent function* that he activated through creative writing reconciled the conflicted aspects of his unresolved nature and freed him from himself, which he illustrated with artistic brilliance in his stories "The Short Happy Life of Francis Macomber" and "The Snows of Kilimanjaro."

Hemingway was aware of the redemptive power of writing, which is why he felt that a writer who squandered the short time he had for writing committed a sin for which there was no forgiveness; and he tells us why with his dying writer in "The Snows of Kilimanjaro" who committed a sin against himself by betraying his talent for the pleasures of the good life that his successive wealthy wives gave him.

Hemingway said this was his most autobiographical story, and I'm led to believe this was how he assuaged his guilt for depending on his first wife Hadley's yearly stipend when he stopped reporting for *The Toronto Star* to write his stories and enjoy his life travelling, and how he betrayed Hadley's love for his second wife's wealth to secure the financial security that he needed for stress-free writing but which also introduced him to the good life that threatened his prodigious talent; and Harry's self-betrayals in "The Snows of Kilimanjaro" were the unforgivable sins against himself that Hemingway dared not speak out loud.

And I'm also led to believe that Francis Macomber's manipulative wife was inspired by his second wife Pauline Pfeiffer, whose rich uncle paid for their luxurious home in Key West Florida where Hemingway did most of his writing and who also financed the African safari that inspired *Green Hills of Africa* and the two stories that transformed the facts of the same safari into literary art.

Was that why "The Short Happy Life of Francis Macomber" was his favorite story, because through the redemptive power of his *transcendent function* he salvaged Macomber's honor and absolved himself of the guilt he felt for living off his wife Pauline until he was able to pay his own way in life? And was that why he resented his third wife Martha Gellhorn whose fierce sense of independence and irrepressible need to make her own name took her away on journalistic assignments from their beautiful home *La Finca Vigia* in Cuba where he wanted her to stay and be the devoted wife that took care of the great writer's needs?

Hemingway wanted it both ways, and he had a lot of issues to resolve because of all his betrayals and self-betrayals and selfish wants and needs; but no matter how much he engaged the redemptive power of his *transcendent function*, he could never resolve the issues of his *shadow* self; and he died a broken man.

29. Wall of Despair

The saddest people in the world are those that have been brought as far as life can take them in the evolution of their individuality, because the longing in their soul for wholeness and singleness of self cannot be satisfied by life and one does not know what to do to fill the hollow in their soul and be the person they are destined to be, like my high school hero Ernest Hemingway. No matter how much life he experienced, he never seemed to get enough; like marlin fishing in the Gulf Stream, which so tested his manhood that he had to prove himself over, and over, and over again and in the process winning trophies and adulation that fed his massive ego which in turn demanded more attention, a never-ending cycle that drove the great author to despair and suicide.

Since my return to Hemingway, I've become acutely conscious of how much time he spent wallowing in self-pity, threatening suicide whenever he failed to get his way with the women he pursued and loved, and how often he made reference to the deep empty feeling in his soul that fueled his depression; and as much as I abhor this callow behavior in my high school hero, I have to admire his endurance.

I've learned many things about Hemingway's life that I did not know before my return to the writer who got under my skin in high school with his deceptively simple style that both excited my imagination and frustrated the hell out of me; but the thing that stood out the most for me now was how devilishly clever he was in his craft of writing, a genius that he began to cultivate at the *Kansas City Star*.

He was only eighteen when he reported for one of the best newspapers in the country, and his eagerness to be the best writer that he could be opened up the pores of his mind and he soaked in all the knowledge that the *Kansas City Star* could give him on the craft of writing, which was considerably more than most writers learned in a lifetime of writing and which can be summed up in a single sentence: learning how to write with clarity.

Hemingway became obsessed with the implications of this precious piece of wisdom, and he devoted all of his attention to learning how to write with the simple clarity of the true sentence; and when he and his new bride Hadley moved to Paris (instead of Rome where he wanted to go) on the advice of the writer Sherwood Anderson, he soaked up everything he could about writing from Gertrude Stein, Ezra Pound, James Joyce, Scott Fitzgerald, Ford Maddox Ford and every writer who had a special talent that would help him hone his own distinctive style; and then he graduated to the great painters to learn the secret of their art, finally settling on Paul Cezanne whose art held a secret that he finally discerned and applied to his writing and which he claimed to be his "secret" that he came to call his iceberg theory of writing that he only revealed after he established his career.

"If a writer of prose knows enough about what he is writing about he may omit things that he knows and the reader, if the writer is writing truly enough, will have a feeling of those things as strongly as though the writer has stated them. The dignity of the movement of iceberg is due to only one-eighth of it being above water. A writer who omits things because he does not know them only makes hollow places in his writing," Hemingway wrote in *Death in the Afternoon*; and of all the things that he had learned about the craft of writing stories, this was the cleverest.

My return to Hemingway brought me back to his biographers, and half a dozen new books which expanded my horizons on my high school hero's life; so when I re-read his stories I could see what he was leaving out, which I could not have discerned the first time I read them, and I had to smile to myself at how much effort he had to put into his stories to IMPLY the soul of his story to give it the impact of a Cezanne painting, like his deceptively simple story "Hills Like White

Elephants" which is all about abortion that is not mentioned once, and this made my literary mentor a devilishly clever writer who found his way to literary fame not by talent alone as he wanted the world to believe, but by the cunning of his writing.

Like most alpha males, Hemingway was a taker and a user; and when he got what he needed from those that served his purpose of advancing his literary career, he discarded them. Like he discarded his friend Sherwood Anderson who introduced him to the literary society of Paris by writing the young Hemingway letters of introduction for Gertrude Stein, James Joyce, and Sylvia Beach who owned the bookstore and lending library *Shakespeare and Company* where writers had a place to meet and talk; Hemingway wrote a novella called *The Torrents of Spring*, which was a spoof on the world of writers and a parody of Sherwood Anderson's novel *Dark Laughter*, because the budding writer wanted to assert his own style.

His wife Hadley called his parody "nasty" and felt it was unfair to their friend, considering everything he had done to help advance his writing career; but the image of having his own distinct voice was much more important to Ernest Hemingway than his friendship with Sherwood Anderson with whom he had been compared when his first book of stories *In Our Time* came out, but he used all his friends this way; and it wasn't a coincidence that the fashionable Pauline Pfeiffer, who worked for *Vogue* in their Paris office and insinuated herself into the married couple's happy life, thought *The Torrents of Spring* was brilliant and praised the budding novelist whom she would inveigle from Hadley and make her future husband, thereby setting the pattern of the great writer's self-destruction.

In my quest for my true self I read hundreds of books and studied many spiritual teachings, and with every book that I read and teaching I studied I initiated myself deeper into the mysteries of life; but it wasn't until I discovered Jung (or, to be perfectly correct about how life works; the merciful law of synchronicity brought the great psychologist into my life because I needed his guidance), did I begin to put into perspective everything that I had learned, because of all the people that I had studied, including Gurdjieff who could do no wrong for me despite all the negative stories that I had read about his life, Jung was the only person who stood far enough from life to see it with a clarity that satisfied my need to know.

Just as Hemingway's stories gave us a verbal portrait of life like Cezanne's art, which initiate the reader into a deeper truth of life, so too did Jung paint a portrait that helped to explain the mysteries of life that I had been initiated into (not quite, but most mysteries; that's why Jung came to me in a dream later in my life to discuss my book *The Way of Soul* to learn everything he could about the alpha and omega of the self); but the difference between my two heroes was that Hemingway could not break through the wall of despair that his life of self-indulgence had brought him to, and Jung managed to do so. That's why they were brought together for this memoir, so I could bring clarity to the *enantiodromiac* principle of life.

Hemingway and Jung were the same insomuch that life had brought them as far as it could take them through the natural process of individuation, and they achieved great success in life; and then they both hit that wall of despair when the momentum of their individuation came to a sudden stop because life could do no more to satisfy the longing in their soul for wholeness and singleness of self, and the difference between them was that Hemingway got stuck on this side of the wall while Jung broke through and realized wholeness and singleness of self. But why did Hemingway get stuck in his despair and Jung break free?

This is the mystery of life essentially, and every philosopher and spiritual teacher and writer and poet and artist in the world has tried to solve it; but because life is an individual journey, no one can solve it for us because there is only self-initiation into the mysteries of life. So at the risk of stepping off my precipice once more, let me see if I can shed a little light on this beguiling mystery.

When I stepped off the breakwater with my *Royal Dictum* intact, which I had vowed to live for the rest of my life but which I did not have to because it served its purpose three and a half years into my journey of self-denial, I promised myself to build my life upon the truth of my own experiences and not sycophantically embrace the truth of others—regardless how brilliant they were; and I went out into the world with what the mystic poet William Blake called a *firm persuasion*—a magnificent theme that the poet David Whyte evolved into a philosophy of life that he expounds upon in his book *Crossing the Unknown Sea, Work as a Pilgrimage of Identity,* and which I put to practice when I left university and started my own house-painting business to make a living and "work" on myself with Gurdjieff's teaching.

"To have a firm persuasion," writes David Whyte, "to set out boldly in our work, is to make a pilgrimage of our labors, to understand that the consummation of work lies not only in what we have done, but who we have become while accomplishing the task" (*Crossing the Unknown Sea,* p. 5).

Who we have become? That's the key to the philosophy of a *firm persuasion*; and in my return to Hemingway, my high school hero whose *firm persuasion* to be the best writer of his generation shone like a beacon in the night, I was forced to see that the consummation of his work had made him a world famous author so true to his craft that generations of writers have been inspired by his writing, but it also made him a tragically flawed man who could not rise above his own despair and he became an alcoholic and miserable bastard impossible to get along with—a "closet everything," as Truman Capote called him in his book *Dance of the Chameleons,* that spoke to the dark, repressed, conflicted *shadow* side of Hemingway's personality that he projected upon the world.

I don't know exactly when Hemingway hit his wall of despair, but he was certainly aware of the deep empty feeling in his soul when he wrote "A Clean Well-lighted Place," and unable to overcame his despair set him apart from my other hero who took the bull by the horns (Hemingway would hate me for this metaphor) and transformed his life by forsaking the trappings of success that Hemingway embraced all the more tightly as he grew in mythic stature and worldly fame.

"He whose desire turns away from outer things, reaches the place of the soul," writes C. G. Jung in *The Red Book*. "If he does not find the soul, the horror of emptiness will overcome him, and fear will drive him with a whip lashing time and again in a desperate endeavor and a blind desire for the hollow things of the world. He becomes a fool through his endless desire, and forgets the way of the soul, never to find her again. He will run after all things, and will seize hold of them, but he will not find his soul, since he would find her only in himself," and which Hemingway valiantly attempted to do while writing his most consummate work of art on man's struggle with himself in his novel *The Old Man and the Sea* after making a total ass of himself in the eyes of the world with his obsessive desire for a nineteen year-old girl who became his model for Renata in *Across the River and into the Trees*.

I can imagine the humiliation that Hemingway must have suffered when what he considered to be the best novel of his career revealed to the world in the great writer's hubristic vaunt of art his obsessive fascination with a besotting nineteen year-old aristocratic Venetian girl—not unlike the celebrated writer Gustav von Aschenbach's obsession with the besotting aristocratic Polish boy Tadzio in Thomas Mann's novel *Death in Venice* which Hemingway had read but failed to mention to maintain his cleverly crafted image of originality in his writing—and which was savagely panned by the critics who called *Across the River and into the Trees* the worst novel of his career. The American writer and highly respected literary critic Alfred Kazin felt embarrassment, even pity, that so important a writer could make such a travesty of himself; and Hemingway's futile efforts to defend himself only dug him deeper into the hole of his humiliation; and Lilian Ross's untimely profile in the *New Yorker* of the badly dressed eccentric writer who liked to lecture people in bizarre Hemingway-speak while drinking champagne early in the morning only added to his shocking disgrace. But when the dust settled enough for him to collect himself, I saw my high school hero reflecting upon his disgrace with the spiritual sobriety of a repentant monk secreted in his cell whipping his sinful soul; which explains the two books that he was reading to redeem himself while writing *The Old Man and the Sea* that garnered him the Nobel Prize for Literature: *Dark Night of the Soul*, by St. John of the Cross, and *Imitation of Christ*, by Thomas A. Kempis.

I have no doubt today since my return to Hemingway that my high school hero was a tormented soul who had to write to save himself, but he could not help himself; his *shadow* had gotten away on him, and he had no control when it came out and took over his ego-personality. Unlike C. G. Jung, Hemingway had become a hopeless victim of his own desires, and his implacable *shadow* crushed his soul with the unbearable despair of his own *nada;* and when he came out of the Mayo Clinic where he was taken again for his depression and paranoid delusions of persecution, he made good on his threat of suicide and blew himself to hell like he wanted to do to his own father so long ago in his story "Fathers and Sons."

30. Hemingway's Secret Way

In the introduction to his book *The Inspired Heart*, the ascetic artist Jerry Wennstrom said, "I hold true that the path lived attentively is a sacred path, and that the fundamental spirit is alive, well, and deeply esoteric. As does any spiritual path, art has the potential to deliver us into our own true *becoming*, which is identical to our world's becoming. Art expresses and defines the deep and collective spirit of our time." Ironically, art wasn't enough for Jerry Wennstrom; and to satisfy the deep longing in his soul for his true *becoming*, he abandoned his art and surrendered his life to a "higher good" which he felt was infinitely wiser than himself.

"I trusted a higher good that I sensed was much better equipped to inform my choices than anything I had available in the limited range of will and intelligence," he wrote, and he burned all of his artwork and gave everything he owned away and for fifteen years surrendered his life to this higher good, and he reconnected with his inner self so deeply that he went back to doing art—just as Katherine Mansfield had concluded, that she had to become more to be a better writer.

"I was dying of poverty of life," Katherine Mansfield said to her husband John Middleton Murry in a letter from the Gurdjieff Institute; and so was the artist Jerry Wennstrom dying of poverty of life. "Art began to feel like a trap to me, yet I was afraid to let go of it. After much praying for guidance, I was finally able to destroy what I had created," he wrote in *The Inspired Heart*; and he stopped painting and gave away his possessions and became a celibate and nourished his impoverished soul with the inherently self-transcending energy of his own becoming that he realized in his unconditional surrender to a higher good, which speaks to the deepest mystery of the individuation process that puzzles all writers and artists.

The dilemma of the *enantiodromiac* principle of life is that it cannot satisfy the longing in our soul for wholeness and singleness of self; the most that life (the natural process of individuation through karma and reincarnation) can do is bring us to that point of self-awareness where we become acutely conscious that we are responsible for the consequences of our actions, and learning how to make the right choices determines whether we can break out of the prison of our own karmic destiny—which sets my two heroes apart: Hemingway choosing the way of selfish desire, and Jung choosing the way of unselfish service to life.

Like Jerry Wennstrom, whose art could take him no further on his journey to his true self which forced him to give it up and surrender to a higher good to show him the way out of his conundrum, so too did I surrender to a higher good when I came to a dead end with Gurdjieff's teaching of "work on oneself." But unlike Jerry Wennstrom, whose unconditional surrender to a higher good brought him back to the way of art, my surrender to a higher good brought me to the realization that my higher good and I were one; and that made all the difference in the world.

This was the single most important discovery in my search for my true self, because in my realization that my higher good and I were one I *knew* with gnostic certainty that my own life was the path to my true self; and I went back to Gurdjieff's teaching with the enlightened awareness that my own life was the way and not Gurdjieff's teaching, as such—nor my *Royal Dictum*, nor the sayings of Jesus, nor Socrates, Sufism, Taoism, Buddhism, nor any other path that I studied or would study, including the ancient spiritual teaching of total awareness that had been brought out to the modern world to re-introduce man to his spiritual self and which I lived for more than thirty years after I dropped Gurdjieff's teaching; and at the risk of stepping off my precipice again and inviting the ridicule of incredulity, let me relate the incredible experience of how I initiated myself into the impenetrable mystery of how to resolve the *enantiodromiac* dilemma of life...

"How can I be certain that the decisions I make are the right decisions?" I asked myself one day, four or five years into Gurdjieff's teaching; but I had no answer. *"I can't be certain,"* I replied, to my horror.

This haunted me for months, because every path that I studied professed to be the right way, the true way, the most direct way, and some even the only way; but my study of philosophy at university had convinced me that one's truth was a matter of personal perspective which depended upon many things; this was why the great philosopher Lord Bertrand Russell, whose book *Why I Am Not a Christian* seduced many people with its iconoclastic charm, could hold one point of view one decade and the next decade hold the opposite point of view, and he backed up both points of view with seductively convincing logic; that's when I began to smell something rotten in the state of Denmark, and I dropped out of university in my third year.

What was rotten was that the mind could not be trusted; that's why I embraced Gurdjieff's teaching—because it grounded me in the reality of personal experience; and the more I "worked" on myself with his teaching, the more certain I was of the truth of my own experiences. That's how I "worked" myself out of the fantasy world of my own mind—and, to my surprise, out of the great minds of everyone that I admired and respected; which taught me to trust my own judgment. And then I asked myself the dreaded question, and I had to find a solution to my dilemma.

As I said, I thought about this for months; and then out of the blue I heard myself say, "Let go and let God." This is an expression I had read and heard uttered many times, especially by devout Christians; but how does one know that one would be letting God in their surrender? How could they prove that it was God?

Letting go and letting God presupposes a phenomenal faith that God will guide one's life; the kind of faith that the disillusioned artist Jerry Wennstrom had to have. But a curious thing happened when Jerry surrendered to this higher good— which he also called "the Universe," as in "letting the Universe take care of me," and which I simply called God—he began to experience unbelievable and timely coincidences which addressed his daily needs; and for fifteen years the Universe took care of his daily needs for survival with the merciful bounty provided by synchronicity, which he relates in his amazing memoir *The Inspired Heart*.

Many years after I found my true self I saw Jerry's synchronicities as another proof that this was how the omniscient guiding force of life guides us through life, always showing us the way when we're in need of guidance; but the trick, of course, as Jerry and I came to realize, is that one has to be open to this guidance. And herein lies the story of my experience of letting go and letting God.

"What if I flip a coin and let the coin decide for me?" I asked myself; but only God knows why I would ask such a foolish question. But the more I thought about it, the more enticing the thought became; and I finally convinced myself that God would be my decider in my flip of the coin. And so began my unbelievably courageous (some would say completely mad) experiment of letting go and letting God, which I did for about six months before I brought it to closure.

"Heads I do, tails I don't," I said to myself, every time I had to make a difficult decision; and then I had to follow through with what God decided for me in my flip. As I said, I had to trust that God was my decider; but I did not call upon God to decide for me in my small decisions whose consequences I could handle. I exercised my own judgment for those decisions, because they did not require "omniscient" certainty that would relieve me of the responsibility of failure.

I lost out on a possible romance because my coin said no when I let God decide for me, and it hurt me emotionally because I had deep feelings for that young lady; but my experiment would have been hollow had I not been true to the flip. And then something happened. Something that defied the odds and rational explanation.

It was happening all along, but I only noticed it about two or three months into my experiment; I began to notice a peculiar "coincidental factor" every time I flipped my coin to make up my mind for me: whenever I had a big decision to make and couldn't figure out what to do but felt in my gut what I should do, my coin confirmed my gut feeling. This was very strange; but every time I got that gut feeling for what I should or should not do, my coin agreed with me. So if my gut said yes, when I flipped my coin and said "Heads I do," my flip agreed with me; but if my gut said no, when I flipped my coin and said, "Tails I don't," my flip agreed with me also. It was beyond belief, but my flip always agreed with my gut feeling!

This defied the odds and scared the hell out of me. But to prove what I suspected was happening, I decided to let my coin decide for me in my small decisions as well. As always, I had to think my decisions through first. I had to figure out what would be the best way for me to go, only then would I give it to my gut and let the coin decide for me; and this scared me also—because my coin always agreed with what I felt was the best way to go, once again defying the odds!

"What's going on?" I asked myself, and I stood back to figure it out; and the more I thought about it, the more sense it made to me in that strange and mysterious kind of way that only a mystic poet like Rumi would understand: as long I trusted my own judgment in my decisions on which way to go, it was confirmed by my flip of the coin; and this led me to my "philosophical conclusion" that God's will and my will were one and the same will; and years later when I creatively explored this bold experiment in my intensely autobiographical but completely fictional novel *The Golden Seed* to get to the deeper

truth of my odds-defying experience, I concluded that my experiment was merely a very courageous and fool-hardy way to make a deeper connection with my inner self—just as I was to learn that Katherine Mansfield did by abandoning literature to "work" on herself at the Gurdjieff Institute and Jerry Wennstrom did by dropping art and surrendering his will to a higher good.

That's why I always had such deep respect and admiration for my high school hero and literary mentor, despite all of his character flaws that I grew to hate the more I got to know about him, because Hemingway had the courage to risk failure every time he stepped into the ring of life, which was why he was so damn competitive in everything that he did—fishing, hunting, boxing, drinking, and especially writing, as he loved to show by shadow boxing with the best writers in the world; and my return to Hemingway proved this feeling, because looking at his life with fresh eyes as I re-read his stories and all the new biographies I saw that he gave his all to whatever he did— especially to every woman he fell in love with.

Whether it was the right decision or not didn't really matter; what mattered was that he was willing to put it all on the line, which gave his writing an authentic ring of truth that transcended space and time but which proved to be disastrous to his emotionally-driven life, as his decision to leave Hadley when he fell in love with Pauline Pfeiffer which he regretted for the rest of his life, and pursuing the blonde beauty journalist/author Martha Gellhorn (Hemingway had a fetish for blonde-haired women, which excited him all the more when cut short like a boy's) when his marriage to Pauline began to sour; but Hemingway always acted on his emotions.

"You don't need big words to express big emotions," he replied to Faulkner's taunt, trusting his own creative genius; but the problem with big emotions is that they can lead to big problems, as Hemingway was to learn over and over again—like falling hopelessly in love with a nineteen year-old virgin which he tried to dignify by making her the heroin of his Venetian novel but which only proved to the world that he had become his own besotted fool; and he had to work like a bastard to write *The Old Man and the Sea* to reclaim his shattered dignity.

Hemingway always set himself up for the conditions of his own suffering, which Jungian therapists today call "the shadow effect," because my high school hero had no control over the dark side of his personality. That was the tragic flaw of his basically decent character, which Debbie Ford expresses with clarity in *The Shadow Effect* (co-authored with Deepak Chopra and Marianne Williamson): "If we don't acknowledge all of who we are, we are guaranteed to be blindsided by the shadow effect." But Hemingway was too egotistical to admit that he could be wrong, and he gave his *shadow* all the material to work with to destroy his life; and it brought him to his tragic end because it destroyed his connection with his inner self.

Hemingway established a firm connection with his inner self when he clocked in his ten thousand hours of apprenticeship in Paris, as he tells us in his memoir *A Moveable Feast*. In "A Good Café on the Place St. Michel" he tells us that he found a nice little café to work in because it was a warm and a wonderful place to write in the bad Parisian weather, and he ordered a *café au lait* and took out his notebook and pencil from his coat pocket and started to work on one of his Michigan stories.

He doesn't give us the title of the story he is writing, but it had to be one of his stories when Nick Adams comes home wounded from the war but the war is not mentioned, based upon his new theory that he had just discovered from Cezanne; and he writes and drinks his *café au lait* and then orders a rum St. James; and a girl walks into the café and sat at a table near the window. He could see that she was waiting for somebody, so he went on writing his story. And the apprentice says: "*The story was writing itself and I was having a hard time keeping up with it. I ordered another rum St. James and I watched the girl whenever I looked up.*"

Hemingway loves the look of the girl and wishes he could put her into his story, but he can't because he knows she's waiting for someone and doesn't belong in his story; but he writes: "I've seen you, beauty, and you belong to me now, whoever you are waiting for and if I never see you again, I thought. *You belong to me and all of Paris belongs to me and I belong to this notebook and this pencil,*" and he goes back to writing, and he "entered far into the story and was lost in it. *I was writing it now and it was not writing itself* and I did not look up nor know anything about the time nor where I was nor order any more rum St. James," (*A Moveable Feast,* p. 6, Italics mine).

Only another creative writer would see the distinction that the apprentice made between *the story writing itself* and *the writer writing the story,* a distinction so vital that it speaks to that mysterious connection the writer makes with the *transcendent function* of his inner self; and Hemingway connected with his higher good as he wrote his Michigan story in that café that day, and this connection with his *transcendent function* was Hemingway's reward for clocking all those hours to become the writer that he wanted to be. That's why he loved to write more than anything else in his life—because it was Hemingway's secret way of becoming his true self, and he honored his secret way more than anything else in the world; which he confirmed by saying, "I belong to this notebook and this pencil."

When a story writes itself, the writer feels he has lost control of his story; but because the story is coming out so well he doesn't dare stop the flow and goes on writing. But at some point the writer and his creative unconscious become one, as Hemingway tells us; and the writer now writes the story that the creative unconscious provides for him; the two wills becoming one in mystical union.

When the writer becomes one with his creative unconscious, he has made that mystical connection with his *transcendent function* that resolves the writer's unconscious with his conscious self, thereby setting the writer firmly on his own individual path to his true self. This is the magical power of the creative process that all writers and artists experience, and it all depends upon their connection with their inner self. That's why

Hemingway sank into the deepest pits of despair when he revealed to his young friend Aaron Hotchner that he could not make that connection with his inner self after they gave him shock treatment at the Mayo Clinic for his devastating depression. It didn't matter that he didn't write; what mattered was that he knew he could write, but he couldn't, and that drove him to suicide.

The apprentice went on to become the great writer that he wanted to be, but he paid a dear price to get there, which he would have gladly renounced for Hadley's love when he took the measure of his life; and his death was tragic. But that's the nature of *enantiodromia*, which can only take us so far on the journey to our true self; and it takes great moral courage to choose the path of unselfish service to life over the path of selfish desire, as my hero Carl Jung chose to do. But I'm glad that I came back to Hemingway, because his life confirms what Jung confirmed for me, that "this life is the way, the long sought after way to the unfathomable, which we call divine. There is no other way, all other ways are false paths." It all depends upon the choice we make when we come to the crossroad of our life—do we choose the path of selfish desire, or the path of unselfish service to life?

———

OTHER BOOKS BY OREST STOCCO

Do We Have An Immortal Soul?

Stupidity Is Not a Gift of God
Spiritual Musings – Volume 3

Tea with Grace
A Story of Synchronicity and Platonic Love

Letters to Padre Pio

Jesus Wears Dockers,
The Gospel Conspiracy Story

Old Whore Life
Exploring the Shadow Side of Karma

Healing with Padre Pio

Why Bother?
The Riddle of the Good Samaritan

Just Going With the Flow
And Other Spiritual Musings

Keeper of the Flame

My Unborn Child

What Would I Say Today If I Were To Die Tomorrow?
Reflections on the Life of a Seeker

On the Wings of Habitat
A Volunteer's Story

About the Author

Orest Stocco was born in Panettieri, Calabria, Italy. He immigrated to Canada and studied philosophy at university. A student of Gurdjieff's teaching for many years which opened him up to the Way, his passion for writing inspired such works as *Stupidity Is Not a Gift of God* and *Healing with Padre Pio*. He lives in Georgian Bay, Ontario with his life mate Penny Lynn Cates. His personal dictum is: life is an individual journey.
Visit him at: http://www.oreststocco.com
Spiritual Musings Blog:
http://www.spiritualmusingsbyoreststocco.blogspot.com

ME AND MY SISPHYEAN ROCK

www.ingramcontent.com/pod-product-compliance
Lightning Source LLC
Chambersburg PA
CBHW031841090426
42741CB00005B/311